92

A View From TheTub

An Inspiring and Practical Guide
To Working From Home

by Millie Szerman

January, 2000

*Thanks for your
help on my journey — :*

Millie Szerman

**Stairwell
Press**

409 North Pacific Coast Highway, No. 900
Redondo Beach, California 90277-2870
310•798•2748   Fax 310•798•8950
www.stairwellpress.com

Szerman, Millie
A View from the Tub: An Inspiring and Practical
Guide to Working from Home
written by Millie Szerman.

p.   cm.
ISBN 0-9672483-7-X
I. Title.   II. Title: A View From the Tub

Cover Photo: Theo Westenberger,
New York City, NY
Cover Design: Pam Gram,
Just Your Type, Chatsworth, CA
Book Design: Taylor Barnes,
TBD Design, Venice, CA

Distributed by
Midpoint Trade Books

10 9 8 7 6 5

Stairwell Press
409 North Pacific Coast Highway, No. 900
Redondo Beach, California 90277-2870

DEDICATION

To my mother, Helena Berkowitz, a holocaust survivor, who taught me that if I did something I truly loved, I'd always be successful, and if I wanted something done right, I'd have to do it myself. A fantastic professional role-model, she was the epitome of home-based entrepreneurship. With only a fourth-grade formal education, her ambition propelled her. A very successful home-based realtor for nearly 30 years, she died in 1981, at the age of 58.

And, to my daughter, Holly Goldstein, for her unending help whenever I need it, and whose encouragement continues to champion my causes. May she know the joy of self-fulfillment.

And to all those who have thought about, maybe even attempted to work from home. It's never too late to fulfill your dream—it just takes longer for some of us!

Table of Contents

ACKNOWLEDGMENTS

Though my mother, Helena Berkowitz, always insisted that "nothing is done right unless you do it yourself," it does take more than one person to complete a project with as large a scope as this one. There are a myriad of individuals who cross our path over the years. And certainly each and every one of them adds or alters something in our perspective. To those individuals whose talents have added to my life (and even those who have taken something from it), I am truly grateful, for you have helped mold the being I am today!

Indisputably the positive energy of those around me, encouraging my success, are first and foremost, and obviously too numerous to mention here. However, I would like to pay specific homage to just a few who worked side-by-side with me through the months of trauma, stress and day-to-day pressures, and without whom, this book would never have gotten off the ground. Please know that these gifted individuals are also home-based!

First, to Carrie, who started off as a Chesloff, and who got married in the midst of all the writing/editing, to become a Rossenfeld: I am deeply appreciative for her writing, organizational and editing talents. And more importantly, for her professional and personal friendship!

To Penelope Paine, who encouraged me from the first to "do it myself," and kept me in-line with information and deadlines. A delightful individual who really knows her stuff!

And, to Taylor Barnes, who at the last minute pulled me through—with her design and calming skills, in the midst of last-minute pressures.

I am indebted, too, to the people at Money Magazine, who thought enough of me and my home-based business success to run the cover story in March, 1996. It spurred a boom in home-based employment. And to the countless eager personalities with whom I spent an infinite number of telephone hours discussing, mentoring, and encouraging them to "do their own thing." Thank you!

To my dear friends (in no particular order): Annie Monk, Ronnie Marks, Wendy Pratt, 'Butch' Weiss, Sherri Cann, Jerry Sue Hooper, Sue Harrison, Susan Williams, Donna Sciortino, and Linda Peretz—with whom I shared my stories, my ideas, my successes and my failures... and they're still my good friends! I am blessed to have you in my life!

I would be remiss not to mention Danny Sonners, a truly talented and magical man who ended up on the wrong side of the law. If he had not gone astray, he would still be a motivating force in my life. It was he who encouraged my home-based journey in the first place, and for this, I shall always be thankful. Perhaps I'll still write a novel or a screenplay about that chapter in my life!

And of course, to my family—my daughter, Holly Goldstein; my brother, Bernie Berkowitz, his wife, Marcia, and my nephew, Michael; my step-mother, Muriel Berkowitz and her daughters, Gail Marshall and Donna Barnes and their families. To Grandma Rose (who celebrated her 99th birthday this year—a tribute to longevity), and to my 'god-mother,' Paula Diamond, a tribute to strength and endurance. To my Dad, Irving Berkowitz, and my 'god-father,' Harry Diamond, both of whom are on another plain, standing proud of their daughter. They all play (and played) a most important part in my life and help keep me focused and dedicated.

As with most of us, I, too have always looked for meaning in life. In the writing of this book, and all that went into my home-based success, I think I've discovered a purpose to my existence: that of a mentor, a teacher, a tutor. I so enjoy sharing my home-based work experiences—the feats and the foibles—with others on their journey. I sincerely hope this book inspires you to be the success you know you are!

Millie Szerman

FORWARD

There's More Than One Way to Skin a Cat

Now that working at home has become an accepted practice in the business world, the category of "home-based" has spawned several subsets of legitimate business people who make a living within their residences. The most obvious subset is the home-based entrepreneur—someone who has left the traditional work environment to begin a self-run venture. But this is not the only type of home-based worker who can benefit from *A View From the Tub*. Anyone who designates time, space and property to working at home can consider themselves "home-based" and can learn something from this book.

The first, most obvious home-based group is the independent contractor—those in business for themselves who choose to set up a home-based office over renting outside office space. Such business people may spend very little time in their offices because their line of work requires them to go to their client's places of business or homes (such as a masseuse or a home inspector), or they may spend the bulk of their time in their offices (such as an architect or a freelance graphic artist).

Still others remain connected to the traditional work environment, but do at least 50% of their work in their homes. Many corporations, in recognizing the value of their employees, are offering the flexibility that allows these employees to telecommute, doing their jobs outside of the office setting. Whether a family relocation, parent/child situation or simply convenience are the motivators, these people, too, have chosen the work-from-home lifestyle. They may be accountants or sales representatives, writers or realtors, but they do not own the business. Nonetheless, they still face many of the same questions, fears and concerns of the entrepreneur and independent contractor and can also gain tremendous benefits from the information in this book.

While it was still a work in progress, *A View From the Tub* had been subtitled 'An Inspiring and Practical Guide to Starting a Home-Based Business.' But in the writing, I realized just how many other work circumstances take place in the home, as well. I knew then that I wanted to make this a broader-based guide for all types of work-at-home situations. For this reason, I changed the subtitle to "An Inspiring and Practical Guide to Working From Home." I recognize that some of the information in these chapters may not apply to everyone, but a great deal of it will. I invite you to read it all, absorbing what works for you and ignoring the rest, as you see fit.

Of course, I can't promise you overwhelming success. But I will pledge that you'll discover aspects and solutions to working from home that you may not have considered otherwise, whether you've just begun thinking about taking the leap or have been at it for years. Whatever your circumstances, I hope you'll enjoy *A View From the Tub* and will want to refer it to others who are about to embark on that home-based journey.

"Be absolutely determined to enjoy what you do."

— *Gerry Sikorski*

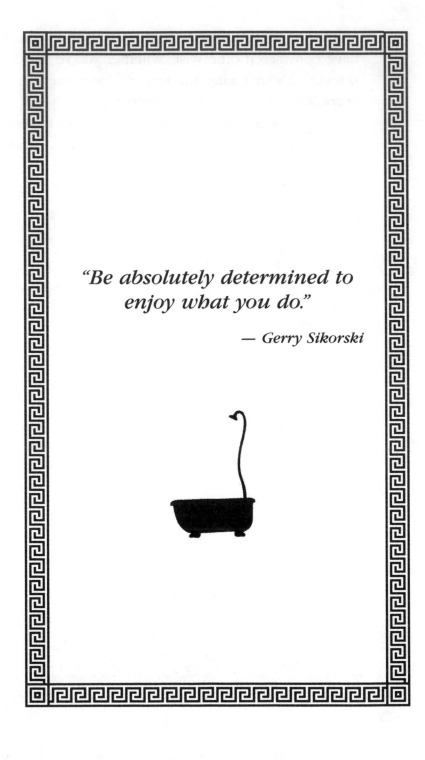

Are you cut out to work at home?

For a great number of reasons, home-based businesses are today's answer to the traditional working life. Once seen as frivolous, fly-by-night endeavors, the home-based office has gained considerable cachet in the working world. With such supply outlets as Staples and Office Depot opening up all across the country and technology allowing "the virtual office," starting a home-based venture can be as easy as printing up business cards and making a few phone calls. Starting a *successful* home-based business, however, requires a bit more internal work and preparation. That, in large part, is what this book is about.

First, let's look at the reasons people become home-based. There are as many reasons for becoming an at-home entrepreneur as there are types of home-based businesses. I like to think of the "whys" as belonging to one of two different boulevards: necessity and choice.

If you've been downsized from a corporate position, can't find work in your field and don't have the financial wherewithal to rent outside office space, you may be enticed by the work-at-home trend out of "necessity."

Perhaps your family or health situation requires you to stay at home, or maybe you don't own a car or live near public transportation. For you, working at home is your only option.

The second boulevard for arriving at a home-based business is by "choice." Theoretically, you could work outside the home, but you'd prefer not to. See if you identify with any of the following statements: "The commute is killing me." "I have all this space at home not being used." "I need to spend more time with my family." "I hate my office environment." "I can't stand the picky things going on with my co-workers." "I never get anything done at the office." "I bring work home anyway." "I'm not appreciated." "I need flexible work hours." "I like my space." "Think of the convenience!" If any of these statements strikes a nerve, then working at home would be a conscious choice for you.

It's also possible that you're currently working outside the home and decide to telecommute, either for any of the reasons mentioned above or because you need or desire to live in a location that makes commuting inconvenient or even impossible. Telecommuters can either become home-based workers by choice or by necessity.

Case Study

NAME: Craig Albertson
BUSINESS NAME: Craig Albertson Mobile Mechanic
TYPE OF BUSINESS: Auto Repair
Established: 1977

OCCUPATION BEFORE BEING HOME-BASED:
Was working for a seafood distributor.
REASON FOR BECOMING HOME-BASED:
Craig began his auto repair business "on-the-side," doing it full time when its income exceeded the income from his full-time job.

For an interesting twist on the home-based business, Craig Albertson takes his auto-repair business on the road. Working for 22 years as a mobile mechanic, he travels to his customer. The biggest advantage to this approach is also a lesson in financing. By eliminating a "storefront" for his business, Craig successfully works with very little overhead. His truck maintenance, license and insurance are his only fixed expenses. All parts are purchased as needed. Craig advises all those starting out to "keep a tight control on your overhead." He also advises you to start your business part-time, if possible, to allow you time to generate an adequate income. As he puts it, "I have seen businesses fail even though they were doing everything right. The biggest problem was that they did not have enough time to develop it."

Craig has a strong Christian faith and a big benefit of this business is that he gets to "meet, talk and witness to lots of people." He adds that "it is very rare not to run into someone I know while I'm around town." Craig's business is successful entirely by word of mouth. He tells that he is now repairing cars for the grandchildren of his first customers. This repeat business adds to the pleasant work environment.

Retirement is expected in the next three to five years for Craig, but he adds that he will "probably always be playing with something."

Often, the decision to work at home starts out as a necessity and becomes a choice. For instance, back in the '60s, many people hosted home parties, where they demonstrated and sold products to others in their neighborhoods. The success of these parties for companies such as Avon, Jafra Cosmetics, Princess House Crystal, Tupperware and a slew of others allowed women, in particular, to run very lucrative businesses from their homes, being there when their children got out of school. That was the beginning of the home-based business. It started out of necessity— the need to bring a few extra dollars into the household without working rigid 9-5 hours—but became an enjoyable social activity that was entertaining as well as profitable.

Similarly, you may begin to work at home because there's no suitable alternative, but later discover that you love it and are more productive as a home-based worker. You may wonder how you ever managed to drag yourself into an office everyday, why you spent so much time buying "career clothes" and worrying about climbing the corporate ladder? When your commute is ten seconds rather than 45 minutes, it's easy to get hooked on the work-at-home lifestyle.

All of these are good reasons to choose a home-based business. But whether you arrive at your decision out of necessity or choice, you owe it to yourself to do a few more mental exercises before deciding to take the plunge. That's what we'll cover in this chapter.

Yes, Virginia, there is a work-at-home personality.

I'm going to tell you something that may discourage you: Not everyone is cut out to work at home. In fact, quite a few people who embark on "the journey" to a home-based business really have no business doing so. Now, I know there is a lot of evidence that supports home-based work—the coming of the Information Age, the precarious nature of corporate positions, the nation's growing respect for small businesses, etc. But the truth is, only certain people have what it takes to work at home—whether they make arrangements with their employer or start a home-based business (from now on referred to as an HBB). What we're going to do in this chapter is determine if you're one of those people whose personality suits working at home successfully.

In order to make that determination, I'm going to take you through a series of steps that will force you to examine yourself carefully. The steps are not difficult or time-consuming, but they do require you to be honest and thorough. So, get a pad and pencil, find a quiet, comfortable place to sit where there are no distractions, and we'll begin.

The first thing you have to pay attention to is what you know. What are you knowledgeable about? In all the years you've been living and working, what have you learned? Do you have a knack with words? Are you good on the telephone? Is your forte bookkeeping, carpets, plastics or vitamins? In our power-hungry society, knowledge is power; so, the more you know about a particular subject, the more power you have in the world around that subject.

So first, you need to figure out what you know, then relate it to your intended business. If you're extending your corporate environment to your home, you might already know everything you need to. But if you want to take that knowledge and go out on your own, you may need to know how to do different things. Does your current knowledge apply to that business?

STEP 1. Write down the words "I know about ———," or "I know how to ————." Now, finish the sentence with respect to your intended home-based business. For example: "I know how to bake the best chocolate-chip cookies in the world." Write down everything you know that would be related to running that business: Buying the equipment, purchasing ingredients wholesale, designing the packaging, setting up a sales force," etc.

Doing this exercise will not only begin to define for you what your strengths are (like creating graphics, dealing with people, negotiating for the best price), but it will also identify your potential business as a *product* or a *service-based* business. There are vast differences in running each type of business, but there are also lots of similarities. We'll discuss these later.

Were you able to complete Step 1? If so, great! You've already laid some important groundwork. If you were completely stumped and couldn't write one thing down, don't be discouraged. You may be focusing on the wrong business, or else you just have more work to do. Move on to the next step, and we'll explore a little more.

Now, the next question is: What don't you know? If knowledge is power, then the absence of knowledge is a weakness. Before you can even think about starting a home-based business—or any business, for that matter—you must be honest about your weaknesses and diligent about strengthening what you can. But you can't strengthen what you can't identify, so that's the next step.

STEP 2. Write down the words "I don't know _____," and finish the sentence with respect to your home-based business. For example: "I don't know how to print up labels" or "I don't know how to sell cookies at retail." Write down everything you don't know that would be related to running that business, no matter how seemingly insignificant.

6

Maybe you don't know how to write a business proposal or market your product. You might not have a clear idea of who can use your product or service. Perhaps you don't know what your potential competitors are doing and aren't up on the latest techniques or technology required to run your dream business.

Be honest about what you don't know. Are you weak on some basic principles you need in order to run the business? Are you unsure about how to get started? Who will your clients be? Will this idea even work? Write down whatever you don't know that may in some way affect the success of your business. And remember: The more honest and thorough you are now, the less trouble you'll run into down the road when your weakness catches up to you.

One of the biggest problems people encounter when starting a home-based business is that they start it without knowing what they're doing. For example, many people buy a multilevel marketing business, and they're so excited about the prospect of making money that they don't ask themselves what they need to know about the business in order to make it successful. So, look at your answers to Steps 1 and 2, and ask yourself these questions: Is somebody willing to pay me for what I know? Do I know enough to make money at what I know? If the answer to either of these questions is anything but yes, head straight to Step 3.

STEP 3. Educate yourself. When I first started my public-relations and marketing business for the gift, stationery and related industries, I knew there was a need in the market for what I knew. I'd had a very

7

strong background in sales, marketing and advertising, having worked for such corporate conglomerates as General Electric, Grey Advertising, Interstate United and Geyer-McAllister Publications. Just prior to starting my business, New Directions, I had sold advertising space in a major trade publication in the gift industry. One of my advertising clients was new to the industry and knew very little about it. After I gave her the benefit of my knowledge, she remarked at the depth of my industry experience and suggested that there might be others who could benefit from my know-how. A light bulb went on.

O.K., so now I knew I had knowledge; what could I do with it? Who needed what I knew? By answering this question, I identified my market: gift manufacturers. Now I needed to present my knowledge in a way that would most effectively benefit them. I asked them some questions. What could I do to help them increase their business and their exposure? In listening to their answers, I recognized a need for a public relations liaison between the product manufacturers and their marketplace.

But I had never done public relations. This was a definite weakness. How could I serve as a liaison if I didn't understand what a liaison does? So, at age 42, with a daughter in high school and no visible means of support, I went back to college at night to learn the technical aspects of public relations. Recognizing my lack of knowledge and doing what was necessary to combat it were among the bravest, yet most important steps I took in order to prepare myself for success.

Case Study

NAME: Leah Flores

NAME OF BUSINESS: Still undecided. Will probably keep it simple and use Leah Flores, Bookkeeping Services.

ESTABLISHED: Began the exploration process in May 1999

ESTIMATED ANNUAL INCOME OF BUSINESS:
Projects an average of $35,000 to start

OCCUPATION BEFORE BECOMING HOME-BASED:
Bookkeeping and customer service.

REASON FOR BECOMING HOME-BASED: "Several jobs have fallen through due to circumstances beyond my control."

Leah is currently working independently for two companies and hasn't officially opened a home-based business, but she's exploring the possibilities of starting one. She is also employed part-time as a bookkeeper in a CPA firm.

"The part-time job allows me the time to explore opening my own business, and I will be learning more of what I need to know while being paid," says Leah. "It also helps a lot that this employer is generous enough to pay for health insurance!"

After hearing from many people over the years that she should own her own business, Leah began to consider it a viable option. "But it wasn't until I heard myself say to a friend, 'I'm tired of other people messing up my employment—I can do that all by myself!' that I realized it was time for me to explore that possibility," she says. After her last employer filed bankruptcy, after Leah had only been employed for three weeks, she started to think about self-employment from home in earnest.

Leah recognizes the importance of educating herself about her field and about running her own business from home. Taking a smart approach, she is looking at all aspects of embarking on the journey, including whether or not it's right for her. "First I have to focus on the short-term and answer the question: 'Do I really want to do this?' Signing up clients will be the biggest challenge for me—'selling myself' does not come naturally. My goal is to generate an income large enough to pay my bills and have 'play' money left over."

9

Now it's time for you to be honest about your knowledge or lack thereof. If you wrote anything at all down for Step 2—and you should have—you owe it to yourself and your business to learn what you need to know. That doesn't mean you can't learn while you're starting your business. Sure, it may be time-consuming and costly and require energy and concentration beyond what you're used to, but remember this: running an HBB is not like anything you're used to. Now's the time for you to prepare yourself for a new kind of life, a new way of working and living. If you approach it the right way, the road ahead will be a lot smoother and a lot more fun.

Following Steps 1-3 will help you carve out the bedrock of your business. It will help you decide if you have the skills for a service business or a product business. It will also help you identify if your skills are marketable and if there's a need for the type of business you envision. If so, it's time to move ahead. If not, it's time to go back to Step 1 with a new vision in mind.

Case Study

NAME: Carrie Rossenfeld
NAME OF BUSINESS: self-titled
TYPE OF BUSINESS: Freelance writing and editing
ESTABLISHED: 1997
ESTIMATED ANNUAL INCOME OF BUSINESS: $30,000 to $50,000
OCCUPATION BEFORE BECOMING HOME-BASED:
Managing editor for a trade magazine
REASON FOR BECOMING HOME-BASED: "Two reasons: In order to be with the man who is now my husband, I moved across the country and left the publishing capital of the world for a city practically devoid of publishing positions. I decided to start a home-based

business so that I could eventually be home with my children and still work."

A self-defined Type A personality, Carrie has learned to be flexible in both her work and her home life. Leaving a fast-paced editorial position in a large company for life in a new city, working at home was difficult for her at first.

"I really missed being around people, and that first year of being on my own was hard," she says. "I also wasn't sure how to structure my time, since I was so used to timing my work hours according to the corporate environment and the train schedule!"

Oddly enough, the Internet has been one of Carrie's favorite social and business tools. She often garners and submits assignments via e-mail, which means she can work with clients literally anywhere in the world without ever having to meet face-to-face. "I also like the Internet because it allows me to keep in touch with friends and family back home," she says. "I've even made some new friends all across the country through websites that interest me, and have had the pleasure of meeting some of them. This is really important because my options for meeting people in a new town while working at home are fairly limited."

Shifting the focus of her business was an early challenge for Carrie. Initially, she had intended to become an outside licensing consultant, an area of expertise at her previous position. "Even though I knew the industry very well, I soon realized that I hated what was involved in doing this type of work. I like seeing the physical results of my efforts, and I just wasn't getting that from consulting. Even though it doesn't pay as well, I love to write, so I decided to pursue a life-long dream of a freelance writing business. Now, I'm much happier."

Carrie advises knowing how to separate your personal and professional lives and setting clear parameters for yourself and your clients. "Be flexible, but know what you can and can't stand before accepting an assignment. And make sure your client knows exactly what he can expect from you for the fee he's paying."

Currently expecting her first child, Carrie will soon face new challenges in her career and home life. "My goal is to maintain the business after my baby is born without feeling overwhelmed or letting it go entirely. I need to work a 'maternity leave' into my business, just as I would if I were working for someone else."

Once you've uncovered any gaps in your knowledge about the subject you're going to base your HBB on, it's time to look at your personality traits. You may not think that personality has anything at all to do with working at home, but think of it this way: It's your personality, your attitude toward life—I call it your attitudometer!—your perspective, your problem-solving approach, that determines the choices you make. When you run an HBB, the choices you make directly affect the success or failure of your business. Therefore, your personality significantly influences your business.

The title of this section, "Yes, Virginia, there is a work-at-home personality," comes from my firm belief that you need to have certain personality traits in order to be able to survive the ups, the downs, the triumphs and the failures of running an HBB. That doesn't mean that if you don't have these traits, you can't be a home-based worker, but the obstacles will be much more difficult to overcome and the struggle may not be worth the rewards.

So, what are the personality traits of the successful home-based businessperson? There are many useful ones, but I've honed it down to four that are truly essential. They generally run in this order:

I. PATIENCE. What's your patience level? Do you frustrate easily? How willing are you to do what it takes? How willing are you to face an empty computer screen or to make that cold call? How willing are you to face the frustration of whatever you are trying to accomplish each day? If you're low on patience, watch out for the day when everything goes wrong: the computer eats your files, no one's returning your phone calls, a check you were expecting doesn't arrive, your deadline's just been cut short by a week, your supervisor at corporate headquarters wants those reports today and your printer broke down. A low patience level can make you want to cash it all in on days like these, and it may affect your dealings with important clients and vendors. Your reaction to a day like this may just make or break you. Do you have the patience?

2. FLEXIBILITY. Do you need to work 9 to 5, five days a week, or can you work 11 to 7 Monday through Thursday and all day Sunday? Do you need a month's notice on all your projects, or can you do a bang-up job on a three-day deadline? What kind of structure do you need? Running an HBB is a double-edged sword: you don't have to report to anyone, but you're often the only one who can get the work done. Some months, the work keeps on coming in; others, you're twiddling your thumbs. Consequently, your schedule may go in fits and starts by necessity. Do you have the flexibility?

3. DISCIPLINE. Can you get up in the morning and go into the area that's your office and organize your thoughts and workload so that at the end of your day (or whenever you stop), you've truly accomplished something? Discipline means not being distracted by the television or the laundry or the household errands that have to get done (because, after all, you're home all day anyway, right?). It means not getting so wrapped up in one project that you forget about the project that's due today or the fact that you haven't eaten in 15 hours. It means being a self-starter, as well as a self-stopper (more on this later). Do you have the discipline?

4. MOTIVATION. When you work for someone else in an outside office, you're expected to give 100% of your energies, creativity, know-how and attention. Sometimes you give more, and sometimes you give less. But a home-based business requires more than 100% of you nearly always. It's you who picks yourself up when everything's going wrong and the last thing you want to do is the one thing you *have* to do. You're the force behind every success and every failure. You make it happen—or not—each and every day. Do you have the motivation?

Check your attitude at the door.

I've always had a positive attitude, and I don't easily get depressed. That probably makes me unlike most people, but it's been a gift to me. My vivacity is infectious: so much so that people often call my answering machine just to hear my enthusiastic voice message! You could say that I have a high "attitudometer."

That's different from being arrogant about your business. If you're patient, flexible, diligent and motivated, but you have a "you're stupid if you don't hire me or buy my product" attitude, eventually no one will buy your product or service. The successful home-based worker understands the difference between a positive attitude and an arrogant one: the former can take you to the moon; the latter can land you in the gutter.

Your attitude can make the difference between feeling like you have no choices and choosing to do what needs to be done. Say you were laid off from your company and can't find work in your field because you're overqualified. You realize that you have to start your own business in order to make a living. You could take the attitude that you're still angry about being laid off and bitter about the Catch 23. Guaranteed, most of the people you market yourself to will pick up on your attitude and be turned off by it. However, if you decide to "make lemonade" out of what you've been given and embark enthusiastically on a brand-new work-at-home career, your potential clients will be more likely to perceive your positive attitude and self-confidence and give you their business. What's more, you'll be happier taking the latter perspective than you would taking the former. You could be more successful than you'd ever dreamed—and live a lot longer, too!

There's an old prescription that I subscribe to called the "smile adage." Basically, it says, even if you don't have anything to smile about, look in the mirror and put a smile on your face. Without fail, you will begin to smile for real, if for no other reason than the silliness of the Cheshire Cat grin on your face. And when your smile is genuine, your attitude improves, as well.

Running a work life in your own home can be an emotional high. Knowing that you're directly responsible for your work success, that what you do really does make a difference, is incredibly rewarding. But the way you approach it matters. Having an HBB requires some major self-evaluation. If you need those "atta-boys" from co-workers, clients or your family, forget it. An HBB is no place to get them. There are no awards, no gold watches for longevity, no unsolicited bonuses. That's not to say you won't get some "warm fuzzies." A job well done is still a job well done, but the person you'll need to rely on most heavily is yourself.

Unmasking the All-Knowing Entrepreneur (or Superpreneur)

As we saw earlier in this chapter, when you start an HBB, it's important to identify what you know as well as what you don't know. However, sometimes you won't know what you don't know until you're actually faced with it. One of the most valuable lessons I've learned in running an HBB is when to admit I'm in over my head. Look at it this way: You wouldn't go to the Supreme Court without an attorney. You wouldn't go to the IRS without an accountant. You have to recognize when you need help and have the humility to ask for it.

Many home-based entrepreneurs are big on control. It's one of the reasons they became home-based in the first place: to maintain ultimate control over their livelihood. The problem is, they think they can do it all themselves. Take mailing services. I can't tell you how many times I got into my car and drove an hour-and-a-half each way to take film to the lab when I could have saved myself the time and spent $8 for an overnight service like Fed Ex, UPS, Airborne Express or others. That's part of the controlling personality. We think, "I don't need any help; I can do it myself." But the truth is you can't do it all yourself. Whether it's putting together a piece of equipment you're not familiar with or menial clerical work like organizing your supply closet, you need to know when to ask for help. If you're doing your filing at 2 a.m., exhausted, or spending your day on administrative work instead of what your clients have hired you to do, then it may be time to get some help.

Also realize that you won't know everything there is to know about running your business from day one.

There is a definite learning curve that every entrepreneur faces, no matter how business-savvy or experienced in the working world. Take Linda, a freelance writer. When she landed her first major project—ghostwriting a book proposal—she took great care in calculating her fee. What she didn't do was ask her client for 30% of the fee up front. A month into the project, elbow deep in revisions and resentment, Linda still hadn't been paid a cent. She soon learned that asking for money up front is standard procedure for many independent contractors.

Case Study

NAME: David T. Gering
BUSINESS NAME: The Gering Group
TYPE OF BUSINESS: Marketing and Public Relations
ESTABLISHED: 1985
OCCUPATION BEFORE BEING HOME-BASED: Corporate executive
REASON FOR BECOMING HOME-BASED: The flexibility and better work environment were key, as well as the opportunity to be able to help with his children.

Are you comfortable in your skills? Do you have any qualms about moving out of that comfort zone? David Gering advises that you must be willing and able to step out of your comfort zone to successfully manage your business. Many do not realize it at first, but when you have a small business, you "must also have a split personality." In addition to working at the service you provide, you will also "work part-time at everything else required to get the job done." This means that you must network, maintain relationships, keep financial records, produce literature, design web sites, and many other tasks. David emphasizes, "You need all of these skills, and if you are lacking, you need to be willing to develop them."

He also provides some good financial advice to those just setting up an office. He believes that the area to spend, or invest, is in equipment. "Buy technology until it hurts and save elsewhere." Because David's business in marketing and public relations requires professionally produced products, he "spent a fortune on his computer." However, he cautions "not to invest too much money setting up your office." For instance, he started with solid core doors as his work areas instead of a desk. The doors provide large work areas and a lot of storage space at a fraction of the cost of a desk. David can now afford to purchase "nice" office furniture but since he rarely has clients into his office, he prefers his "inexpensive" furnishings.

OK, so you're a self-starter, but are you a self-stopper, too?

Being a self-starter and a self-stopper are personality traits that are essential for the successful home-based worker, but I've pulled them out of the general list because I feel they require special attention. Being a self-starter is directly related to all four of the traits mentioned: patience, flexibility, discipline and motivation. Being a self-stopper is only related to one trait: discipline.

Self-starters have a plan. They know what they need to do in order to get themselves going, and they have the discipline and motivation to do it in the first place, plus the patience and flexibility to work around whatever obstacles might block their path. Whether it's setting their alarm clock for 6 a.m. because they need to make a phone call to the East Coast, or making sure their desk is clear at the end of the day so they can start fresh in the morning, self-starters come through without poking or prodding from anyone else. If you're a self-starter, you don't need to rely on anyone else to put the immediacy of work upon you.

Self-stoppers also have a plan. They know that they need to achieve a balance between their work life and their personal life, and they know where to draw the line. Self-stoppers don't work 23 hours a day and forget about everything else. They recognize the importance of rest, recreation and laughter, and they know how to set limits. If you're a self-stopper, you understand that it's just as important to know when to quit (for the day, anyway) and to have the discipline to do so. "Tomorrow is another day" is a credo self-stoppers live by, and one no home-based business-person should live without.

When will you work?

Self-starting and self-stopping have much to do with your hours of operation. Theoretically, you could work 24 hours a day or five minutes a day. In a regular office, even if you don't punch a clock, your co-workers are aware of whether you're in or not. In an HBB or telecommuting situation, no one is there to monitor your time, which means more often than not, you're the warden. You get to decide when you work and when you don't. But before you set your mind on sleeping until noon or knocking off at three everyday, consider your specific situation. I truly believe in the concept of a body clock. Barring any physical illness, you'll find it easier to live your life and you'll be much more successful if you pay attention to your own body clock. Are you used to getting up at 7:00 a.m.? Then keep doing it—that's a major recommendation. If you had the kind of job where you worked 8 to 5 and wished you worked 10 to 8, you may have the freedom to do that. But you may find that the type of business you're in dictates that you work certain hours.

When I first started my business, I found that I still had to be up early. But the difference was, I didn't have to fight traffic to get to a sales appointment, and I didn't have to put mascara on while I was half asleep. I could go to my office in my pajamas and write up a press kit or phone a photographer to confirm a photo shoot. And I found that I was much more productive that way.

What you might find is that instead of spending two hours getting ready for the office, you can now do other things that are productive for your business. By 10:00 a.m., you may have already put in two hours. What a good feeling! You may find that instead of taking a shower in the morning, taking a shower at noon feels better because you've accomplished something and you need to take a break anyway. Instead of struggling on the Lifecycle at 6 a.m., you can go at 2 p.m. because you've already put in a full day. If you want to take a nap in the middle of the afternoon and wake up later to work into the wee hours, you can. Such is the life of a home-based entrepreneur. Telecommuters may or may not have such luxury, but their time will probably be considerably more flexible than it would have been in an outside office.

One problem that home-based workers run across is the way other people disrespect their time. Many business-people think that because you work at home, they can call you at all hours and expect you to be ready, willing and able to service them. Unless you want to be "on call" 24 hours a day, you need to find a way to manage that. Whether it means turning off the business-phone ringer at night or at the very least, screening your calls through your answering machine, you must control your availability to colleagues and clients.

I answer the phone with the name of my business, "New Directions," weekdays between 7:30 a.m. and 6:30 p.m. Any other time, it becomes my home phone, and I answer "Hello" or "Good morning." (Sometimes, I forget that it's the weekend and answer "New Directions" anyway!) This way, when I don't answer in my "business voice," people know that they've reached me "off duty" and are less likely to call after hours again. Whether it's a client who wants to discuss a new product release, or a magazine editor who needs a suggested retail price, they're unlikely to repeat this faux pas.

There are, of course, exceptions to every rule. There might be a project that requires after-hours consultations because you simply can't get to it during the day. When I was the editorial director for one of my clients while she was writing her book, I'd often field calls late at night out of sheer necessity and the importance of the project. But let me emphasize that this is the exception, not the rule.

Case Study

NAME: Rick Cyge and Lynn Trombetta
NAME OF BUSINESS: Meadowlark and Larksong Productions
TYPE OF BUSINESS: Music recording and performing in addition to marketing and talent agency
ESTABLISHED: 1993
OCCUPATION BEFORE BEING HOME-BASED: Rick and Lynn were cofounders and managers of a Museum Store in Arizona.
REASON FOR BECOMING HOME-BASED: After winning an award for the best museum shop, they decided to leave the store and begin a new business. Quickly, they discovered that they were both musicians and began performing.

Lynn states that leaving their secure positions was slightly unnerving, but it also left a void that they were able to fill with their business activities. They strongly advise that you really love what you are about to do because you will "eat, sleep and drink it."

The popularity of the Internet and desktop publishing has greatly expanded their business horizons. Lynn says, "Desktop publishing, the Internet and the services now offered to small business have leveled the playing field." Now, home-based businesses are "more normal" and companies are targeting them to provide services.

Lynn and Rick produce their own literature and promotional pieces, and they are thrilled with the ability to print small quantities. Where in the past you needed to print thousands of a specific piece, now you can print small quantities on your own desktop printer if needed. Lynn adds, "It's wonderful not to have to be locked into specific promotional pieces. Since we design our own, we can always reflect where we are right now." She adds that if you do not have the skills, these services are available to you.

Their last piece of advice is to stay lighthearted and loving. As for potential name confusion, they get calls on their toll-free number for Meadowlark Lemon (from the Harlem Globetrotters).

How many supporting roles can you play?

It is essential that you wear many hats when you're a home-based worker. Unless you have the capital to hire a staff, you're going to be your own bookkeeper, secretary, file clerk, purchasing department and boss. You're probably going to make your own coffee. You'll have no one to bounce things off of, no associates who understand what you're doing or provide camaraderie. Even if you create a network of outside "colleagues," they may not be available when you need them. Loneliness is a common complaint of new home-based workers. You'll also be the one who cleans up your desk, returns your messages and schedules your appointments. You're all you've got.

If you're lucky enough to have a staff, you'll have to learn how to delegate. If you've never managed people, you're suddenly a manager. If you thought you were a great people manager, you may find that you're not so hot. When you start a business, you'll discover everything you're lousy at, but you'll also discover skills you never knew you had. See? You can make a darn good cup of coffee! You'll also discover there's a different rewards system that comes from working at home. It's rare when someone tells you that you've done a good job. In fact, the surprise comes when you're not expecting it. When a client comes in and renews your contract or reorders product or tells you that you've helped to increase their business—that's when the "atta-boys" come. It's rare, but it does happen, that a client will actually tell you, without your prompting, that you're a valuable part of their team.

For me, the "atta-boys" come when I've finished a press kit or when a press release I've written appears in a magazine. The pats on the back don't come the same way they used to, and they're less frequent, but when they do come, it's so much more satisfying than when I was working for someone else. I can take all the credit for a job well done—not just part of it.

My personality has always been upbeat and energetic. Over the years, especially these last ten where I've worked for myself, I've developed a sense of self-reliance and maturity that I believe can only be gained when you do things for yourself. Working at home, supporting myself in a successful fashion, certainly has changed my perspective—both personally and professionally. I can't imagine ever not working for myself in some capacity.

If you've determined that you've got what it takes to work from home, then you can begin writing up a business plan. There are many books on the market that can help you do that formally, or it can be as simple as writing down the 5W's: WHAT your business is, WHO your clients will be, WHERE your market is, WHEN you will break even, and WHY your business will succeed. You might also write down the sixth W: How. "How will I make this work?" This exercise should be adequate for getting you started.

At the end of this chapter (and each one hereafter) you'll find a checklist to help remind you of the points we've covered. Remember, as you go through these steps you may discover that being home-based is not for you, or at least it may not be right as your main means of financial support. If, after careful anaylsis, you're still feeling strong, then carry on.

Believe it or not, you've overcome one of the biggest obstacles to determining whether working at home is right for you. But is it right for those around you? In the next chapter, we will address how your working at home might affect others in your life.

Checklist 1 ✎

✓ ———— Write down what you know and what you don't know as it relates to your home-based business. Be honest!

✓ ———— Take steps towards educating yourself about what you don't know. What are they?

✓ ———— Take a reading of your "attitudometer" and write down the results. Does it need work?

✓ ———— Rate yourself on a scale of 1-10 on the four essential personality traits of the successful home-based businessperson: Patience, Flexibility, Discipline and Motivation. Which areas need work?

✓ ———— Determine if you're a self-starter and a self-stopper. What steps do you need to take to develop each of these areas?

✓ ———— Start thinking about what your hours of operation should be. Are your hours of operation in conflict with the business you've chosen. What else conflicts with these hours? How can you rearrange your day to meet your needs?

✓ ———— Write down the ways you'll set limits for yourself and others in terms of your hours of operation.

✓ ———— Write down the different supporting roles you'll need to play, and which responsibilities you'll need others to help you with.

A View From The Tub...

Notes ✎

26

Notes

"Courtesy is the one coin you can never have too much of or be stingy with."
—*John Wanamaker*

HOW FAMILY, FRIENDS AND OTHERS FIT INTO YOUR HOME-OFFICE SCENARIO

2

U nless you're a monk, important people in your life are going to be affected by your decision to work at home. It doesn't matter how gung-ho you are on the concept—if it doesn't jibe with other members of your immediate world, you could be facing some serious conflict down the road. Better to address it now and forestall problems in the future.

The truth is, being in your own business affects you as an individual as well as the people around you, and working at home intensifies the issues. Family, friends, roommates, neighbors and other businesspeople who aren't used to you setting up shop at home will now have to deal with you there. This transition is not without its potential glitches—but none of these glitches is insurmountable if you approach the situation with respect, compassion and open lines of communication. That's what this chapter is about.

The Pockets of Life
Key to organizing your life to work at home is recognizing that your life has a wide variety of segments that make up the whole. You have a

social life, a family life, a personal life, a business life, a community life—the list goes on. Let's visualize your whole life as a garment—an apron, a jacket, a vest, whatever works for you—with each segment being a pocket in the garment that you can pick from as you choose. In the context of all these pockets, your work life is only one pocket, and its importance changes—certainly daily and often hourly.

Here's a good example of what I'm talking about. When I was working in sales in corporate America and my daughter was in nursery school, I once had an exceptionally long drive to meet a client. When I was finally able to call the office (this was in the days before cell phones!), I retrieved a message that my daughter had fallen and needed stitches. Suddenly, my family-life pocket became top priority, even though I was on the job. These kinds of events happen in spite of our efforts to control our lives.

The fact is, your work life needs to have a pocket in the garment of your whole life. It has a location, a time, depth and breadth, a beginning and an end. What's different now that you're working at home is that you're the one who sets those parameters—and you have to be the one who enforces the rules.

Case Study

NAME: Shirley Cornelius
NAME OF BUSINESS: Shirley Cornelius Secretarial Service
TYPE OF BUSINESS: Provides secretarial, bookkeeping and financial services
ESTABLISHED: 1987
OCCUPATION BEFORE BEING HOME-BASED:
Secretary and Bookkeeper

REASON FOR BECOMING HOME-BASED: Working from home appealed to Shirley because she could be her own boss and make her own hours. "The number one thing I enjoy is that I can work my hours around my family."

The one thing that she would do differently is to hire child care when her son was very young. When she began her business, she attempted to both work and care for her toddler, simultaneously. According to Shirley, "it would have been easier to focus on one or the other, but not both."

She also brings some valuable financial advice. Stating that she has seen many fall into this trap, she advises, "don't get caught up in spending a lot of money up front. Use discretion at the outset before investing in equipment, supplies, and incurring marketing costs. A much better plan is to make these purchases as your business grows." Some of her clients are her previous full-time employees.

Looking to the future, Shirley plans to keep her business at a level that allows her to maintain her flexibility. She "wants to make enough money without going crazy."

It's all in the family

Part of the beauty of working at home is that you're more readily available to your family than you ever were. And, of course, there are positives and negatives to this situation. Suppose your spouse has to go on a business trip and wants to take you along. In the past, you might not have been able to take time off from work, but now that you're the boss, you may be able to do that, after making a few arrangements, of course. Remember: this is still a job, and you've made a commitment to your success. Because we're in an increasingly electronic age, we can, in fact, do things we weren't free to do before, and working at home is one of those things. This is the upside to being home-based.

There can be a downside, however. Suppose your spouse—or other people in your life, for that matter—start to take advantage of the fact that you're home most of the day. Perhaps your family expects you to run more errands for them. Or maybe a neighbor asks you to take care of their dog while they're away. If people expect you to do more non-business-related activities now that you're working at home, they may not be giving your work its proper regard. If it means being a hard-nose and having a family meeting, or politely (but firmly) denying the neighbor's request, then that's what you have to do. If one of the reasons you decided to work at home was to be more available to your family, then you can definitely make that plan a reality. But you'll need to set limits. Your family and friends must understand that sometimes you can't chitchat on the phone just because you work at home. You can't always run errands because you have a job to do and goals to reach each day. You can't take in your neighbor's dog because it's disruptive to your business. Whatever the conflict may be, you need to communicate your needs and feelings clearly to those involved and set limits for these requests and expectations. Show them that you take your business seriously, and they will, too.

Guilt may raise an ugly head here. You think, "Well, I'm home, I can go pick up the cleaning." But what if 5:00 p.m. comes and you still haven't picked up the cleaning? Will you feel guilty because you were "home all day," or will you realize that you were working and you have a legitimate reason for not picking up the cleaning? Will your family have the same realization?

Working at home, as flexible as it can be, almost necessitates more structure than working outside the home. It certainly requires a strong constitution. People around you who are not trained in the ways of the home-based business are not going to understand your structure. The solution is communicating what the structure is and sticking to it.

Case Study

NAME: Brian Lawrence
NAME OF BUSINESS: Sell the Bride
TYPE OF BUSINESS: Provides business, sales and marketing consulting to the wedding industry; publishes and sells marketing publications for the wedding professional; and maintains a wedding-industry resource website.
ESTABLISHED: 1998
ESTIMATED ANNUAL INCOME OF BUSINESS: $75,000
OCCUPATION BEFORE BECOMING HOME-BASED: Continues to serve as marketing director for an invitation manufacturer
REASON FOR BECOMING HOME-BASED: Additional income and a way to channel the industry knowledge accrued over a 20-year period.

As someone whose home-based business is run in addition to his full-time job, Brian has his work cut out for him. He says his greatest challenge is not letting his business crowd out his family time.

"As you become more successful, a home-based business can be very consuming, and it can take priority over family if you let it," Brian comments. "It is so important to maintain the balance and remember, most important of all, this is your home. Beyond that, it's your place of business."

Brian advises having a designated area and complete privacy when conducting business, especially if your business thrives on telephone contact. "Privacy is not as important when you deal with people face to face. You elicit the human response of having family around you and often that builds rapport with clients."

He stresses the need to establish credibility and gather testimonials, beginning with your first customer. "Do whatever you can to get published and posture yourself as an authority in your field as soon as possible."

Setting the Rules

One way to set structure is to manage your accessibility to the world. At an office, you may have had voice mail or a secretary to screen your calls, or e-mail that you could choose to answer or not. In a home-based business, you could opt for voice mail, e-mail, a cell phone and a pager, so you can be reached at all times. In my opinion, however, this is not a wise idea. Let me explain why.

I absolutely, positively refuse to get a pager. The reason: I am obsessed with staying in touch. I have three phone lines in the house, a cellular phone, voice mail on all my lines, an 800-number to pick up my messages, and e-mail. I am connected, but only when I want to be. I don't have to answer to anybody. My friends, family, colleagues and clients know I'm obsessed about retrieving messages, so it won't be long before I get back to them. But if I had a pager, I would never have a minute to myself. (A small aside on equipment: if you're on the phone a lot in your business, invest in a headset. It will save you hours of aching neck, back and shoulders. And if you can splurge and buy yourself a cordless headset, you'll be in heaven! More about equipment later.)

The point is, if I had a pager I couldn't organize the pockets of my life and it would be chaotic. For you, a pager may be a godsend, particularly if you're afraid to go out the door in case you miss an important call, or if you place a high value on your accessibility. The trick is to figure out which systems will help keep your life pockets in place without allowing one to overpower the others. Electronics should help you, not make you its slave.

Now, if you're working from home for another company, you may not have as many choices about how accessible you are. Your employer must be able to reach you during business hours, and he/she may decide that you need to carry a pager or be available for a telephone meeting at 7 a.m. or phone in a progress report at 5:30 p.m. Clearly, these are terms you should discuss with your employer—in fact, get them in writing if you can—before you begin to work from home. Whatever terms you agree upon, you should be no more or less accessible to your boss than a traditional office employee.

Case Study

NAME: Felicity Walsh*
NAME OF BUSINESS: Working from home for a textile company
TYPE OF BUSINESS: Textile designer
ESTABLISHED: 1998
ESTIMATED ANNUAL INCOME OF BUSINESS: $18,000
OCCUPATION BEFORE BECOMING HOME-BASED:
Did the same job part-time on site, with an interstate commute.
REASON FOR BECOMING HOME-BASED: "When the division I work for relocated 1,000 miles away, my supervisor offered me the opportunity to set up an office at home and work part time."

Felicity was in the rare position of being handed a home-based position on a silver platter. She credits the offer to many factors: a long-standing relationship with her company, the fact that she was working part-time, and the fact that her customers were all located close to her home. Although she wasn't specifically looking for it, a home-based position found her.

"I was fortunate to have maintained my relationship with the company even after I left my job to raise my children," says Felicity. "I highly recommend to women who leave the working world to have children that they don't close any doors behind them. You never know what's down the road. Many companies now regularly offer flex time, shared responsibility or part-time employment options, which are ideal for working mothers."

In her case, Felicity had worked as a full-time textile designer for the company for seven years before having her first child. Paring down her hours to part-time, she became a consultant for a year and a half. At three months pregnant with her second child, she stopped working for five years, occasionally doing freelance work for other clients. When Felicity's former supervisor approached her with a part-time offer, she took it, making the commute once again three days a week.

Finally, the home-based option was presented to her. Felicity is now paid by the hour (working roughly 15 hours per week, plus light travel), and while she doesn't have health benefits, she is offered stock options and was able to join the company's 401k plan. She says she's much happier working from home, as are her husband and her children, ages 11 and 9.

"I like being home because I'm much more relaxed, not having to get dressed for work everyday and go to the office," she says. "The tough part is trying to ignore everything that has to be done in the house. Luckily, my office is in a separate room—a necessity because the volume of fabrics I need to store would be an eyesore in the middle of the house. Some people can work that way, but I need the separation."

Despite what seems to be an ideal situation, Felicity admits to having constant challenges to overcome, including feeling isolated from the rest of her co-workers, being interrupted by friends and neighbors, and the most frustrating of all, staying organized. "I'm not the most organized person by nature!" she says. "I'm not rigid and I have trouble sticking to a schedule. Also, when you're not in the office atmosphere, you have a tendency to do more than you would normally, because you feel you have to prove to people that you're really working. There's more pressure to produce."

Felicity has learned to overcome many of these obstacles by staying in frequent touch with her co-workers via telephone, fax and e-mail; plus she visits her main office at least once a month and travels to the new location quarterly. "I like the little bit of travel that I do," she says. "I think I'd get bored if I didn't have that because it adds diversity to the job."

*name has been changed

Kids!

Say Mom comes home from the corporate world and wants to talk to her sister back East. Without fail, that's the moment when the eight-year-old is tugging at her for attention. The same thing can certainly happen when Mom is in her home office on a business call. Whose fault is this and what can be done about it?

I believe that this problem comes from not having or communicating to your children a clearly defined structure for when you are and are not available. A woman I know who works at home and has two school-age children uses red and green paper signs. When the red sign is on her office door, her children know not to disturb her. When the green sign is up, she's fair game. (Tip: If you decide to use this system, have a corollary rule whereby if the red sign has been up for an exceedingly long time and/or the child has an emergency, he or she can knock quietly before coming in—you may have forgotten to take the sign down after your important phone call.)

If you have children coming home from school at 2:30 p.m., that may be a good time to schedule a break for yourself. Don't make any appointments for that time, join them in a snack, play a game. When break time's up, make sure they know it's time for you to go back to work. It's by creating (and enforcing) these rules that you'll avoid having children who feel neglected or feel the need to disturb you while you're working.

If your business permits it, you might try taking a break when the kids come home and picking up again after they go to sleep. The answer is creating a schedule that works for you and your family—one that everyone can live with.

Case Study

NAME: Evelyn Salvador
NAME OF BUSINESS: Desktop Publishing Plus
TYPE OF BUSINESS: Graphic design and professional resume service
ESTABLISHED: 1990
OCCUPATION BEFORE BECOMING HOME-BASED: Bank officer
REASON FOR BECOMING HOME-BASED: Evelyn became involved in desktop publishing while working as a bank officer. After the wave of mergers and downsizing that hit the banking industry, she decided to leave that type of work and provide desktop publishing services from her home.

Evelyn began her business with a common misconception that her HBB would be "all frills." She soon learned that this was not the case and now advises those embarking on a home-based journey to carefully plan their surroundings and schedules to provide a professional work environment. This is especially important when you have children. She discovered that while you can work at home and care for a child simultaneously, you can do neither optimally. Unless you establish clear boundaries, you will have interruptions and your children may feel rejected. Her advice is to "integrate some baby sitting, day care, or camp so that all needs can be met." Also, discipline and routine are key to successfully balancing these two areas of your life.

Evelyn has some key advice for the times when the task of juggling work and family seems daunting. "Try never to feel bad about the compromise you and your child(ren) have to make for your home business. After all," she adds, "when you were away at work, you were AWAY at work, not to be seen until 6 or 7 p.m."

Currently her business caters to those individuals needing "high-end" resumes and businesses requiring self-promotional pieces. Evelyn plans to steer her business more towards larger corporations in the future. She feels that this will allow greater flexibility and creativity, and a less demanding schedule, while also generating a larger income.

Evelyn's motto has served her well. "Envision success until it's achieved and you'll never fall short of your goals in life."

I Need Space!

A common mistake people make when they first try working at home is they set up shop on the family's dining room table. I strongly recommend against this for many reasons on which I'll elaborate later on in this book. For now, I'd like to address how creating a workspace in a common area of the home can affect others who live there.

In order to work at home, you need to create a work area that's absolutely your space. If you're commandeering an area of the house that used to be common, you need to take it away from your family and never give it back. Otherwise, they will not consider your business a legitimate one. It doesn't matter if it's a TV tray or a converted closet—that's your office, no matter what. Regardless of where it is, as long as your family understands it's sacred, it will become yours.

Now, this rule works both ways, of course. Before you nab the den or a corner of the garage, you must hold a family meeting to discuss it. After all, you're taking something away from your family—what are they going to get back? By showing mutual respect, you should be able to reach a reasonable compromise with your family on your work space. It's a communication issue, and communication is the key to most elements of business—and life!

Case Study

NAME: Wendy Pratt
NAME OF BUSINESS: Pratt Public Relations
TYPE OF BUSINESS: Public relations and marketing, as well as book-author and product publicity with a consumer slant
ESTABLISHED: 1996
ESTIMATED ANNUAL INCOME OF BUSINESS: More than working in the corporate sector
OCCUPATION BEFORE BECOMING HOME-BASED: Worked in the entertainment field for 12 years and segued into advertising and public relations in the book publishing arena. Did both agency and in-house public relations.
REASON FOR BECOMING HOME-BASED: "After having been through one or two corporate merger-layoffs, I wanted to have control over my own destiny. My only security was to create my own business."

Wendy's business has grown steadily since she began. "In less than three years, I have been able to more than double my former salary," says Wendy. As her client list grew so did her income which made it necessary for her move. She now enjoys a large office with a private entrance and beautiful garden view.

Flexibility, personal freedom and the chance to pick and choose her clients are definite perks for Wendy, who occasionally misses the camaraderie of a traditional office setting. The tradeoff is more time for quality, productive work with fewer interruptions. "I've always been independent, disciplined and a hard worker," she says. "Having my own business allows me the opportunity to put my talents, abilities, and expertise to work for the authors, publishers, and manufacturers I represent. I am passionate about what I do, and having my own business has afforded me both personal and professional growth."

Wendy advises newcomers to home-based businesses to take risks. "I made the transition from the corporate world to my own business slowly and in stages. I kept a job with a P.R. agency and moonlighted on the side. Within six months, I was able to devote full time to my business. I believe a transition period is ideal for anyone starting out."

She recommends testing the waters, taking some clients/projects on the side, making sure you have set up a comfortable work space. "Moving to my present home gave me a new lease on life and a much larger office!"

A final note of advice from Wendy: Pay people to help make your business run more efficiently and ask successful people for their advice.

Other Household Members

Perhaps you have a roommate—or more than one. They, too, will be affected by your decision to work at home. Believe it or not, it's really much easier to deal with a person who is not a family member living in your house. If you own the house, then it's even easier because you already set the rules. If you share rent, communication once again is key, and you need to consider your roommates' needs and feelings.

Will clients be coming and going when your roommate is home from work and wants to unwind? Will the phone be ringing at odd hours, disturbing his/her sleep? Consider these possible occurrences and discuss how you'll deal with them.

Setting limits on space and time and establishing a structure that will work for everyone in the household should help prevent most work-at-home problems. Everyone's requirements are different, and the type of business you choose will dictate what you need to be successful in terms of your own immediate environment.

Get a (social) life!

When you have your own business or make the switch to working from home, you can often come and go as you please and do what you want to do. Sometimes, you may forget that you need other people—that means making a concerted effort to include others in your life. It's not uncommon for new home workers to become lonely or uncomfortable because the people they're used to seeing all day aren't there. Everyone from the coffee vendor to your supervisor is technically out of your work space.

As a result, the telephone can become a major social stimulus. It can be your lifeline to the outside world, literally. However, you must be careful that the telephone does not replace the people in your life. The phone can become our best friend, but we can't deny that we require physical contact—it's essential.

Perhaps you've had too much human stimuli in the past. In an office, you can be so bombarded and distracted by the stimulation of people around you that you don't finish your projects and you end up taking work home. When your office is at home, you don't have that problem, but you may forget that you need that social outlet. There's no one to remind you to take a coffee break or chat about last night's game or last week's staff meeting. You have to provide these "people/breather breaks" for yourself. It's good not only for your own productivity, but also for your physical well-being and your psyche. No man (or woman) is an island. It's important for us to stay connected to humanity, and not just through electronic means.

When you worked in an office, you probably wouldn't have dared to take the afternoon off to go shopping with a friend—what would your boss think? But when you work at home, you do have that option, as long as you take care of business first. Your outside social life takes on a different meaning when you work at home because you can go play if you want to.

Some people who work at home don't feel entitled to skip out for the afternoon. They lock themselves in their offices from 9 to 5, barely taking five minutes for a bite to eat, much less a quick telephone conversation with a friend. These people feel a sense of guilt: because they work at home, they have to create the feeling that they do, in fact, have a "real job." They may not think other people see them as "real workers." To combat these guilty feelings, they drive themselves like slaves. They don't have the automatic structure of an office environment, so they go overboard in trying to create one for themselves. As a result, they don't give themselves any rewards—those that should come from working at home.

Oddly enough, I see this behavior stemming from a lack of structure, rather than too much structure. Real structure requires balance. It demands the proper proportions of work and rest. If you structure your time correctly, you should be able to go to the beach some afternoons—not necessarily every week, but once in awhile. Why should your home office be exactly like your corporate office without the commute? Here's where you can take a long morning walk—and work late that night. Your favorite store is having a one-day sale and you don't have to squeeze your shopping in during everyone else's lunchtime. With a little planning and organizational skills, you can have fun and still get the job done.

One of the perks of working at home is, if a friend is in town on vacation, you can duck out and meet her for a long lunch and put in the overtime at the end of the day—or start early the next day. You can view time differently now that the time is yours to negotiate.

Weekend? What's that?

Used to be your weekends were sacred. Only now that you work at home, Saturday and Sunday may become work days. The traditional things may not be appropriate now, but that's not to say that you can't make them appropriate. Your "weekend" may not be Saturday and Sunday, but must be penciled into your calendar nonetheless. You can put weekends back into your social life. Flexibility is key here: you have the option of working at night or working on the weekends because the phone won't bother you. It's a juggling act, but again, you set the rules.

When you work at home, you may find that you're not seeing your friends as often because your schedules aren't in sync anymore. Don't let them drift away—take a step back and reach for your friends.

You need to schedule down time. You have to get away from your work so that it doesn't become all-consuming. Your social life has to be a pocket that does get picked! Remember our discussion last chapter about being a self-stopper?

I like to plan social events for during the week and leave weekends for spontaneous fun. Season theater tickets allow me to be social with friends on a scheduled basis so I won't be able to ignore them. You'll find that if you plan things, you'll manage to fit everything else in around them. That way, you can have a social life and not feel guilty about it.

Your extended family

When you work at home, you tend to develop relationships with people in a different way. With the increasing number of home-based businesses in this country, more people are realizing the major advantage of dealing with others who also work at home.

Colleagues, clients and friends who work at home don't mind hearing from me on the weekends or in the evenings—they can always choose not to answer the phone, but they can be available if they're ready to talk business. I've also noticed that many business associates have become social friends. There's a sense of connection that you don't necessarily get when you call an office worker. (Of course, to gain this sense of connection, you have to be confident enough in what you're doing to reveal that you work at home—and if you don't consider working from home a real job, then you have a problem.)

I'm one of those people who makes friends easily. I have no problem getting close to folks right away. I think this helps others feel more comfortable dealing with me as a person, for who I am. Does this sound like you, too? Are you outgoing, gregarious and comfortable around other people? Or are you more reserved and less likely to reach out? If you are normally quiet and shy, it may take more of an effort for you to make friends once you're working at home. Make reaching out to others a conscious part of your day, and you may find you've enhanced more than just your business life. On the other hand, if this is simply not who you are, you may want to re-think this working arrangement. Working at home will isolate you much more than working in a traditional business environment.

People who work at home can make wonderful social contacts. For one thing, they tend to be very sensitive to the personal things that affect business life—like a death in the family, an illness or even El Niño! They seem to have a different sensitivity to catastrophe. Of course, you can't be sharing catastrophes all the time. No one wants to deal with someone whose kid is having a tantrum every time she gets on the phone. But if you're conducting business from your home, you could say your daughter is home with the flu; if you were working in an office, you might feel strange telling your boss you're going home early so you can take your sick daughter to the doctor.

More often than not, when you work at home, you develop closer relationships with your clients. If you're comfortable doing so, at some point you might tell them that you work from home, that you're available after hours or on weekends (if this works for you). You may find that it creates a more personal environment that spawns a more intimate friendship. In this way, you'll make a different kind of friend, and you'll enrich all the pockets of your life.

Is there room in your home—
and in your life—for co-workers?

Deciding to bring someone else into your work-at-home environment requires much contemplation. First of all, whether or not it will work for you depends on what your business does and where it's physically located. It's very easy for me to contract business out, where in a corporate setting, I would have somebody in-house do the work. When I do contract out, I find it's easier to use people who also work at home. With electronic capabilities, it's becoming increasingly easier to do, and if your home office has space limitations, it may be a necessity.

If hiring others to work for you is an issue, ask yourself these questions: What is my business? Is it conducive to having other people do it? What are my space limitations?

Maybe it's work your family could help you with, like stuffing envelopes or collating. Remember: it's okay for your family to help you, but it's also okay for them not to want to. You may get to a place where you're either going to pay your kids to stuff envelopes or hire somebody to come in part time. At that point, the work you contract out becomes a business expense—which is, by the way, tax deductible.

47

If you opt to bring someone into your home-based business to help you out, you need to ask yourself some very important questions:

"How comfortable am I with managing other people?" When you were working for someone else, or in a corporate setting, were you in a management role? Now that you're in your HBB, you're the boss. Do you feel as comfortable managing others as you do managing yourself?

"Can I trust someone to work in my home when I'm not there?" At this point in my life, I live alone, so having another person working in my home will not affect others in my household. However, I live among a myriad of lovely things I've collected over the years. I do have some hesitation about having strangers in my home when I'm not there. These trust issues are virtually nonexistent in a corporate office setting. If your business dictated it, would you feel comfortable leaving others alone in your home? And what about the expectations of the person you're about to hire? Be sure to discuss this aspect with them. You might consider a work agreement that maps out the ground rules, such as hours per week, time off (and notification thereof).

"Am I flexible enough to work with others' schedules?" In Chapter 1, I explained why flexibility is an essential trait of the home-based worker. Here's another way it comes into play. Oftentimes, the people you hire to work in your home have other jobs or commitments. I have a part-time helper who can do quite a bit of work out of my office, but some projects require my supervision. Luckily, she is extremely flexible and is able to work late hours and on weekends. Since my workload fluctuates and her full-time job requirements also shift, she has been a wonderful asset in her flexibility. And because I'm flexible, too, the arrangement works out beautifully. Can you work under these conditions?

Unless you're hiring several people, most often you'll be able to utilize someone as an outside contractor, where they're responsible for their own taxes and insurance. You may have to pay them a slightly higher wage, but you won't have the obligation of employment taxes, workman's compensation and the like. In the ten years I've been in business for myself, outside contractors have worked beautifully for me. (Of course, I issue a tax form 1099 if I pay them more than $600 a year, but we'll cover that more thoroughly in a later chapter.)

Hey, neighbor!

Most communities have legal requirements about working at home that protect neighborhoods from being disturbed by the daily activities of businesses. We'll touch on this subject a little later on in another chapter, but we do need to mention your neighbors, as they are people in your life. It's part of your "community pocket."

· As with friends, your "at home" neighbors might be very curious about your being at home during normal daytime "working hours," particularly if they're used to seeing you trot off to the office in the mornings. Of course, if they work outside the home, they may never know you haven't gone off to an office. If your business requires people to come and go from your home, you'll raise suspicion. (You also might have some trouble with getting a city license—more about that later, too.) Again, communication is key. You might mention to your neighbors that you have a home-based business, and they should expect to see comings and goings. They'll appreciate that you took their concerns into consideration.

You'll want to pay attention to deliveries, too. Perhaps your neighborhood is a very quiet one. Will you have delivery trucks coming and going? They make an awful lot of noise, and the last thing you want is to upset your neighbors. You'll want to consider an outside mailing address (again, we'll cover this in another chapter) for a number of reasons, not the least of which is the delivery issue. My business requires a good deal of shipping and receiving, and my home mailbox would always be overloaded. My solution was to rent a business mailbox at a nearby Mail Boxes, Etc. location. That way, I don't have to worry if I'm not at home, about curious children or neighbors peeking at my packages and mail. And I don't get complaints about noisy vehicles.

Your place in the community
Community life is a pocket that frequently doesn't get picked at all. Years ago, everyone knew their neighbors, watched out for each others' kids and had block parties and bridge nights. These days, as our lives get busier and more complex, we often don't even know the name of the family next door. For the home-based worker, this sense of isolation can be especially devastating.

The good news is, the discomfort of our distance from society can force us to reach out and become a recognized part of our community. Whether by doing volunteer work, participating in town or city events, or even joining the local Chamber of Commerce, you can establish a place for yourself in a wider forum.

If you decide to join the Chamber of Commerce, you'll meet many businesspeople who may be looking for the same type of enhancement you are—business, social, or both. Even if you only attend one meeting per month, you'll get a sense of belonging you could be missing by working at home. Depending on your business, you might also find a new client or two in this arena.

Community events are great places to enrich the many pockets of your life. You may have the kind of business that's appropriate for local street fairs, such as baking, crafting or event planning. You may have a skill that you can take into a senior-citizens home or local hospital. Volunteer to make phone calls or distribute flyers, and you'll continue to meet new people while you're doing something good for your town.

Participating in local events will give you a sense of community from donating your time and expertise. It'll make you feel good about who you are and what you do, but it's also a shot in the arm for your business.

One caveat: Once you begin to volunteer, organizations may take advantage of your charitable actions and disrespect your time, interfering with the other pockets of your life—especially if they know you work at home. The way to avoid this is, once again, to communicate, set limits and enforce your own rules.

Dealing with people is one of the trickiest parts of life, but life wouldn't be worth living if we didn't interact with others. Now that you understand the roles different people play in all the pockets of your life, you'll have an easier time of fitting them into your home-based scenario.

Next, we'll address the practical considerations of setting up an office at home, and the tools you'll need to make the transition a smooth one.

◆

Checklist 2 ✎

✓ ———— List the different "pockets" of your life and the elements of each that are vital to making them work.

✓ ———— Discuss your plans to start a home-based business with your family and other household members. Explore and write down any fears, concerns or potential problem areas any of you may be aware of. Discuss ways to ease these areas.

✓ ———— Write down the equipment/systems you'll need in order to control your accessibility to others.

✓ ———— If you have children, define for them the rules of conduct during business hours and what constitutes an emergency!

✓ ———— Create a plan for your work area that is acceptable both to you and to everyone else in your household. This may be a good time for another family meeting.

✓ ———— Jot down a few ideas for creating social contact during your workweek. Pencil them into your schedule and make them happen!

✓ ———— Think about whether or not you should hire others to help you run your business. If so, is your office conducive to working with others? What type of manager are you? Are there classes at the local adult education or college that can assist you in being a better manager?

✓———— Make friends with your neighbors and let them know that you'll be working at home, especially if there will be a lot of activity that they'll notice. However, do be firm about setting limits on your time and availability should they start to ask for favors!

✓———— Plan some activities that will get you out into the community, whether it's joining the Chamber of Commerce, doing volunteer work or participating in community events.

Notes ✎

Notes ✎

"*Opportunities are usually
disguised by hard work,
so most people
don't recognize them.*"
— *Ann Landers*

PRACTICAL CONSIDERATIONS 3

In the last chapter, I briefly discussed how the people in your life—family, roommates, co-workers, etc.—might be affected by your home office's location. In this chapter, I'll more thoroughly explore exactly what tools you'll need to make that space work for everyone involved.

When you first started thinking about setting up a home office, you most likely pictured the place where you'd spend most of your day—where it would physically be located in your home, what it would look like, how you would arrange the various components. This type of imagining is actually very beneficial because it gets you thinking about the practical considerations of working from home. I suggest you explore your imagination just a little further.

An office in paradise?
When you dream about working from home, do you imagine yourself in a beautiful beach house on a remote tropical isle? Or how about in a rustic wood cabin somewhere high up in the mountains? Your dream might be to run your business from your traveling houseboat. Tempting, isn't it?

Not so fast. Even though you can give up many of the traditional work environment requirements when you work at home, your geographical location must be considered more carefully in terms of accessibility and logistics. Will others (customers, clients, mail-delivery people, repair people) be able to get to you easily? What if there's a power outage, a snowstorm or a flood and you can't work or travel? Will you be isolating yourself even further from friends, family and community?

When I first thought about starting my company, I salivated over the idea of locating it in peaceful, secluded spot at Lake Tahoe, a magnificent picturesque locale in Northern California on the Nevada border. I imagined tranquil work days, surrounded by gorgeous outdoor scenery. Luckily in a way, that winter a series of severe winter snow storms locked Tahoe residents in their homes for days at a time. I quickly realized that I needed to be a little bit closer to civilization in order to assure my business would run smoothly and that I would be safe. Today, I work from my home at the beach. It's away from the big city, but a short walk from a local business district, and it's perfect for me.

Working from home certainly gives you a lot of freedom, which is one of the great allures for so many people. But it doesn't divorce you from the realities of life. I suggest you thoroughly examine the consequences of any extreme location decisions to determine if they're truly practical for your working future.

Where will you sit?
When people first discuss an HBB, they determine that they can set up shop just about anywhere—all they

need is an electrical outlet and a phone line, right? Theoretically, yes. But in reality, they need to consider all the logistics of setting up their home office for maximum efficiency, comfort, and success.

Of course you need electrical outlets, a telephone line, and lighting today. Choose an area where you have a bit of room in which to move around, and at the very least, you'll need a desk or table in that space. People often choose to set up their office in a dining room or an area of the home that's not used very much. Frankly, I don't consider the dining room to be the ideal place for an office, unless you want to stop using it as a dining room and convert the space into an office by closing it off to family traffic. For reasons we've discussed earlier in this book, you need a space that you can call your own—a place that's not a living space for other household members.

Even if you live alone, the last thing you want to do is walk through the room that's your office in order to get to other areas of your "living space." Danger lies in this arrangement because you're forced to walk by all the work you have pending in order to get to other rooms, and you'll be uncomfortably thrust into "work mode" on your down time. Unfortunately, this is a likely scenario when your home is short on office space.

A much better idea is to set up an office in a large, walk-in closet with a door that closes, or to select an area of your home that can be screened off. Perhaps a far-off corner of your garage or a free-standing tool or storage shed will work well, if you create the space as your own. In this way, you won't see your desk or hear your business phone ringing when you're on leisure time—even if, technically, you're in the same "room" as your office.

A photographer colleague of mine even utilized a downstairs bathroom that was not currently being used as her darkroom/office. She covered the sink in the large room with a removable plywood countertop that served as a desktop when the sink was not in use. There are numerous ways to creatively convert unused areas into office space, if you take the time to think about it. A visit to your local hardware, home-products or decorating store should help you pull it together.

Here's a good example of what I'm talking about. A friend of mine (let's call her Nancy) runs a public-relations business out of the dining room of her darling little one-bedroom, over-the-garage carriage-house apartment. Her dining room/office leads into her kitchen. Every time Nancy goes into her kitchen, she gets completely stressed out because she has to trample through her office and see all her unfinished work. Though she has a great apartment and a growing business, she feels overworked because there's no physical separation between her work "pocket" and her relaxation "pocket." As a result, she's more anxious than she'd be if she worked outside her home!

Another friend of mine set up her freelance-writing office in her living room. Her work space was less than six inches from her living space, with no screens or buffers in between. Consequently, she hated being there, even when she wasn't working, and chose to spend her leisure time anywhere but in her apartment. In effect, she trapped herself into using her apartment almost strictly as an office, which is certainly not the goal of the home-based business.

A final no-no on the location of your home office: don't choose the bedroom or it may prevent you from getting a good night's sleep. If you can't avoid it—perhaps you live in a studio apartment—then curtain off either the bed or your work area. And try to avoid working in bed; it will likely cause insomnia and stress.

The physical separation of work and play areas is not only good for your psyche, it's also good for your tax bill. With the number of HBB business people continuing to rise—at last count, more than 42 million people in America have some type of home-based operation—the IRS is being particularly picky about home-office deductions. For example, if the room that holds your office doubles as an extra bedroom, it is not considered a home office, and you could have a tax liability for it. If you have an area that's clearly and solely used for business, you'll find it much easier to make your case for home-office tax deductions. (More on taxes in a later chapter.)

Sharing your space
An ideal situation for those who lack the space and/or funds to set up an office is working in an office that's already set up for someone else. If, for example, your husband or roommate has a home office and works outside the home during the day and at home in the evenings, you may be able to use his or her office during the day. This situation, of course, only works if each of you is respectful about sharing this space. It can get very crowded, if not distracting, to have two people working in an office created for one—

particularly if you're overhearing each other's telephone conversations, using the same equipment at the same time, or leaving each other's work out of place.

Case Study

NAME: Danielle Bradford
TYPE OF BUSINESS: Field sales for Toshiba
ESTABLISHED: 1997
OCCUPATION BEFORE BECOMING HOME-BASED: Senior product manager in the marketing department for Toshiba Corporation.
REASON FOR BECOMING HOME-BASED: "As a corporate marketeer, a large portion of my job was traveling to customers with the salespeople and helping them explain the products. Soon, I was recruited for several different sales jobs. One involved moving from Orange County, Calif., to San Francisco to work from home. I reasoned that, even if I had an outside office, I wouldn't be in it 80% of the time, so it made sense for me to work from home."

Danielle found herself part of a shifting trend in corporate sales: it isn't necessary for many field salespeople to report to a main office since they're visiting customers most of the time. It's more cost-efficient for the company to have those employees work from home than to maintain an additional facility that would remain empty a great deal of the time. This arrangement suits Danielle, a disciplined and ambitious executive, just fine.

"None of my health benefits changed, only my pay structure," she says. "I'm now a commissioned salesperson instead of a salaried worker, which makes me work even harder!"

Danielle understands the need for balance in her life and says her job affords her balance in spades. "I don't have that 30- to 60-minute commute anymore, so I use that time for myself," she says. "I've never been interested in office politics or gossip, which can invade your life when you're working in a cubicle. This arrangement allows me to be very productive and very focused and get my job done between 8 a.m. and 5 p.m. In the corporate environment, I used to work from 6 a.m. to 8 p.m. and still feel like I wasn't getting everything done by the end of the day."

For a time after Danielle accepted her new position, her husband also worked at home as a wine distributor, which necessitated a few house rules. "He knew that if my door was closed, I was working and not to be disturbed. If it was open, he could come in and chat." Danielle also chose as her office a room that was on a different floor of their house than her husband's office. "I knew I would need that physical separation in order to be productive," she says.

Her advice for anyone considering making the move from a corporate environment to working at home is to evaluate who you are and what you need from your work life. "To be the most successful in a field job, you need a little bit of wisdom, a lot of discipline and comfort with yourself. I know people who went out in the field, got lonely and came back to corporate jobs. This would be hard for someone who depends on the office for social networking."

She also recommends examining where you are in your career. "I'm fortunate that I've already had exposure within the company, so I'm not just some name on a sales report. And it can be very difficult to climb the political ladder when you're not in the game. If you want to be in the inner circle, at some point you do have to go back inside. Luckily, I haven't a whole lot of desire to be president of the company, so the tradeoff is acceptable to me."

For someone who a few years ago couldn't imagine life without a secretary, working from home has made Danielle a savvy independent who's now on a first-name basis with the late-night staff of her local Kinko's. But she wouldn't trade her situation for the corner office in a high-rise building. "I so love what I do and what I am. I've made a lifestyle choice that's very fulfilling. My whole focus in life, beyond the day-to-day, is to make sure my sales skills are very well-honed."

Telecommunications Considerations

The telephone, your indispensable home-office tool, prompts other practical questions such as, "How many phone lines do I need?" Like separating your physical work space from your physical living space, there are many benefits to getting a separate business line. And if your business requires a fax machine and/or computer modem, you may wish to set up yet another line.

Twenty years ago, most people didn't require more than one phone line at their home; today, most homes are already wired for at least two (often up to five) telephone lines. When I first started my business, I realized I needed three lines: one for incoming calls, one for outgoing calls and a designated fax/modem line. In order to set up my extra lines, I needed to get permission from the city to bring the lines into my home, and I spent a good deal of money to have the city-mandated physical conduits installed—a process which required that a portion of my front lawn be dug up. Construction people had to dig the hole, and city officials had to approve the construction.

Luckily, this procedure probably won't be necessary for anyone working from home today because it's become common for residences to have multiple lines. However, you will have to pay for any extra jacks installed (a one-time charge) and for service and maintenance of the extra line(s), toll calls and additional services. It's wise to shop around for the most cost-efficient long-distance plan you can find based on your business-calling needs, and any plan that's hooked up to a business credit card you'll use often is a definite plus. This is a great way for you to earn frequent-flyer miles merely from the cost of doing business, and it's a practice I strongly urge you to follow.

I believe that every home office should have at least three lines. For maximum cost-efficiency, as long as your business doesn't require a completely separate line at all times, the business line can be used as a personal line when you're not working. To help keep your records straight, the phone company may offer a service that allows you to track your business calls by dialing in a code before the number you're calling. If you bill your clients for phone calls, you could even arrange the coding system so that each client gets a different code. Check with your local phone company to see what options are available to you.

Here's another practical question about the telephone: "Do I need to be listed in the Yellow Pages?" If your business comes from the general public, and finding you in a reference resource of this type will help boost your business, then you'll have to have a "business-type" phone line service. It will definitely be more expensive than a residential line service in terms of monthly fees and toll charges. However, if you have other means to promote your business, I strongly suggest that you stay in the residential realm. If you alert the telephone company that you have a home-based business, you may be charged more for the same call on your business line than you would on your home line. Save yourself the added expense unless it's absolutely necessary.

If you do decide to be listed in the business directory, you'll want to be listed under the name of your business, rather than your own name. Doing so adds credibility to your business and says something to the world about the nature of what you do. Choosing the right name for your business requires a certain amount of research, thought and possibly legal action. We'll talk more about choosing the perfect business name in a later chapter.

One last word about phones: ideally, you should be able to answer all of your phone lines from anywhere in your home. This will reduce your stress level considerably because you won't have to go running upstairs or from one end of the house to the other in order to pick up your business line—breathlessly. You can always turn off the ringers of the phones you don't wish to answer so as not to disturb you or other family members with loudly ringing telephones.

Case Study

NAME: Marianne Szymanski
NAME OF BUSINESS: Toy Tips, Inc.
TYPE OF BUSINESS: Toy research consulting and publishing of Toy Tips Magazine and toytips.com website
ESTABLISHED: 1991
OCCUPATION BEFORE BECOMING HOME-BASED:
Sales representative for an international toy company
REASON FOR BECOMING HOME-BASED: "I wanted to run a virtual company and manage a healthy family life."

Marianne is constantly on the go and has learned to set up some strict guidelines for herself in order to remain organized and productive. She once ran her business from an outside office, but soon realized how difficult it was to manage the office and run the business, especially when work required her to be out of the office a good deal of the time.

"Because I travel a lot, it didn't make sense for me to have an outside office," she says. "It was a nightmare and a waste of money. Now I hire independent contractors who don't come to my home, and they all report in to me on Friday via e-mail. It's a much better system because I don't have to worry about management;

I just do my thing. You never have to have anyone coming to your home if you don't want to."

Marianne is a staunch advocate of renting a retail mailbox in order to limit interruptions from mail and package-delivery people. She also recommends only checking your e-mail a couple of times a day—first thing in the morning and last thing in the evening—so that you're not constantly getting caught up in answering messages.

When callers dial Marianne's business phone, they hear six options, for which they can press a button to learn more. To check her messages, she simply dials into one voice mailbox. "Sometimes all people want to know is my fax number or address," she says. "This saves time."

Call waiting is an option she avoids, but caller I.D. is a must. "It sounds really unprofessional for clients to hear another call coming through, but if you have caller I.D., you'll know which calls you missed."

Marianne firmly believes in separating all aspects of her business and personal lives, from keeping business papers in her office to shutting the office door at the end of the day and not looking back. "You must be a self-starter and recognize the need to manage both your business and home life in your daily routine," she says.

Finally, she suggests, "Make sure you invest in the best equipment, such as a great computer system that won't break down. Do your homework, and stay up on the latest advances in technology so that you get the best system for your business."

"What other equipment will I need?"

Good question! What kind of business do you have? More often than not, your business will need a computer, probably a PC. As for computer peripherals, the people who sell you your computer will be able to help you more than I. I will tell you that if your PC has a built-in fax/modem, you don't necessarily need a separate fax machine—with one exception: if you rely on your PC to receive faxes, your computer needs to be on in order for you to receive them. If you don't feel comfortable about leaving your computer on 24 hours a day, you can purchase a double plug that will allow you to receive faxes on your fax machine.

If you travel or are away from your desk a lot, a laptop is a major convenience. If it also maintains a docking port, you'll have the option to send faxes directly from your laptop. Many hotels have computer data ports for laptops, though not all have the equipment you may need. A laptop is very convenient, but also an expense you may not need to incur right away.

What you will definitely need is a work surface, preferably a desk, although a dining-room table or folding table will work in a pinch. You'll also need some kind of filing system, whether it's as rustic as cardboard boxes or as corporate as a filing cabinet, and you'll also need adequate storage space. Remember to check out used-furniture stores or local newspaper classified for some great bargains; it's not necessary to spend a lot of money when you're starting your business.

Your equipment needs will change as your business grows, as retailers catering to home-office workers are realizing. Odds are, the moment you buy your computer, for example, it will have become outdated almost before you have it out of the box. To combat this problem, several office-equipment manufacturers now offer rental programs whereby you can rent or lease equipment and trade it in as you need to. I suggest you research these options carefully. Your initial output may be less in a rental situation, but if your lease is long term, you could end up spending more money than you would have had you bought the equipment outright.

Another point about leasing: don't be afraid to approach the vendor about renegotiating your contract, particularly if you've been a long-term customer. When I leased my copier, for example, I negotiated a buy out option at the back end. With months to go on the lease, I mediated a more reasonable buy out for much less than the original contract stated. The truth is, most manufacturers don't want to take back well-used equipment—it's useless to them, unless they can use or sell the parts. Most manufacturers will be willing to negotiate with you if you show interest in buying the used equipment.

One more item you'll want to consider on leased electronics: maintenance agreements. A single visit from a repairman can cost you $300 to $400 in parts and labor. Maintenance agreements for this kind of electronic equipment are very important to your cash flow.

A leased postal machine and postal scale may also be of value to you, depending on your business. In my line of work, where I'm sending hundreds of pieces of mail each week, it's a real hassle to go buy stamps; besides, if I bypassed the long post-office lines and bought stamps at a mailbox center, I'd pay a premium for them. For me, the cost of a postal meter has amortized over time as a very worthwhile business expense.

Other postage options include "Stamps by Mail" and "Stamps by Phone," offered by the U.S. Postal Service, which allow you to have stamps delivered to your door by either filling out a form or dialing a phone number. As for new technology, talk of downloading stamps from the Internet is buzzing, and just coming on the market are electronic devices that attach to your PC to provide and keep track of postage. Find out more about these options by reading the business section of your local paper and trade magazines about home-based businesses.

Some pieces of expensive equipment are worth purchasing, despite their cost. When I first started my business, I paid to have copies made at a local copy house. I soon found that the cost of my time—going back and forth to the copy house—was not worth the monetary savings. The convenience of having a copier at home was well worth the price.

Case Study

NAME: Jennifer Horton
NAME OF BUSINESS: Self-titled
TYPE OF BUSINESS: Freelance writing, editing and photography
ESTABLISHED: 1988 (with full-time jobs in between)
ESTIMATED ANNUAL INCOME OF BUSINESS: $50,000 plus
OCCUPATION BEFORE BECOMING HOME-BASED: Editor of trade journal
REASON FOR BECOMING HOME-BASED: "I love to have a flexible schedule, and I'm a real night owl."

A jack of many creative trades, Jennifer has the chance to try them all, thanks to her self-made home-based business. Her business is flexible, allowing her to write and edit for many different kinds of clients as well as demonstrate her photography skills.

While she has shaped her business into exactly what she wants it to be, Jennifer does have a few hard and fast rules that keep her on track. "Take a shower by 10 a.m.," she says. "Don't answer your personal phone during the day, and post your deadlines on a bulletin board right near your computer so they don't sneak up on you."

Jennifer recommends keeping the volume on your personal answering machine either turned down or turned off during working hours, otherwise you may find yourself in an embarrassing situation with a client on the phone. "One day, I was on the phone pitching a story idea to an editor, and I'd forgotten to turn down the volume on my personal answering machine," she relates. "My friend called at that exact moment and was leaving me a very detailed message about her date the night before. I had to dash to the answering machine to turn off the volume, but the editor had already heard most of my friend's story! Luckily, the woman had a good sense of humor and laughed about it with me, but I learned my lesson!"

Jennifer swears by equipment that makes your job easier, such as a cordless rechargeable headset by General Electric that clips onto a belt loop. "Not only is it a great tool, it forces me to get dressed in the morning!" she quips.

Other advice: "Know that you'll have work before you quit your job. Tell everyone you meet what you do, and carry business cards with you at all times. And you really need to print a specialty on your business card because people need to know who you are and what you do."

As a single woman working in a big city, Jennifer is diligent about making after-hours plans with friends so that her social life remains healthy. "It's not like when you have a job and you go home to someone else. I'm here by myself every day, all day. I really have to go out at night and be with people."

Although her business is strong, Jennifer says one of her fears is that the work will stop coming in. "I wonder every day if this is going to work out. I'm afraid it's going to dry up. But I just keep plugging away, and I'm always thinking about the next assignment."

Your support needs

At some point, you'll want to establish relationships with outside vendors: photo labs, paper houses, photographers—whatever you need for your business. For the most part, you'll have to fill out applications to get credit, but you should also have a dedicated corporate credit card because it will also help you establish yourself. You may want to set up a Dunn & Bradstreet account; it's easy to do. By calling the local D&B agency (or their toll-free number listed in the resource area at the back of this book), you can establish yourself for credit-rating purposes. Being listed in D&B substantiates your business and gives you greater credibility in the eyes of vendors and potential clients.

Certain vendors will allow you to negotiate costs. I have established myself with a number of photo laboratories who bill me monthly at wholesale rates. I bill back my client and charge a 15% mark-up for my time. It still saves the client money by giving them a wholesale rate plus the small mark-up, rather than the usual 100% mark-up they'd pay retail.

A very important point about your relationships with vendors: because you are a small account, you simply must pay them on time or you won't get the service you need when you need it. If you pay your bill on time, you can expect out-of-the-ordinary service. If you don't, you can't expect your vendor to come through for you when you have a rush job. Like it or not, he has an obligation to his bigger clients—the ones who pay him large sums of money each month—and they'll get the quicker, better service. You're just a little guy, so you have to gain power in other ways, mostly by being good to the people who service you.

An outside, off premeses mailbox (not the one at your front door) is another must-have, in my opinion. For privacy reasons, you probably don't want your home address on your business stationery, business cards, letterhead, envelopes and mailing labels. And you will need all of these things if you want to insure the credibility of your business. It's not that big an expense, but it's worth a lot of money in the message it sends to clients about your business.

When shopping for a mailbox, choose a retail mailbox center like Mail Boxes Etc. or Postal Annex rather than a post-office box. For one thing, post offices won't accept Federal Express, United Parcel Service, Airborne Express or any other private delivery service that isn't affiliated with the United States Postal Service. If you expect to receive packages this way, a post-office box will leave you high and dry. Also, most of these centers will give you an access key so you'll have 24-hour access to your mailbox. That means you'll be able to retrieve your mail before or after hours, or even on Sundays—a boon to the home worker.

The one snafu to rented retail mailboxes is the newly proposed (currently tabled) post-office regulation that may prevent you from using a suite number in your address. Instead, your address must read: Mary Smith, Acme Company, PMB 250, 125 Main Street, Anytown, USA. The "PMB" stands for "private mailbox," a tip-off to consumers that they're dealing with an outside mailbox rather than a street address. If you want to maintain a very corporate, professional image, this may be a fly in the ointment for you, at which point you'll have to weigh which is most important: your privacy, the services you receive, or your image.

You may be able to negotiate costs with your mailbox center, particularly if you purchase other services they offer such as stationery, office supplies, copies and mailing. Many of these centers are franchises, as opposed to corporations that have to go by the book. Utilize services like these in your area because they depend on small businesses like yours. They want you to be happy, so you stand a better chance of negotiating with them. A $10 fee doesn't always mean a $10 fee—don't be afraid to discuss it with them.

The same goes for paper houses, express-mail delivery services, Office Depot, Staples and other office-supply stores. Setting up accounts with these businesses establishes your credit and your credibility in the marketplace. Plus, it helps your cash flow if you can pay off your bills at the end of the month instead of COD.

Your banking needs

It's not essential to let the bank know that the account you're opening up is a business account because, like the phone company, some banks will charge you a premium for it. However, you will want to separate your personal financials from your business financials (unless you have a terrific bookkeeper and accountant). There are numerous types of bookkeeping software that will help you differentiate your accounts electronically. But in the physical universe, I recommend having a separate checking account and credit card for business expenses (remember to get a credit card that establishes frequent-flyer mileage). Pay that card and your vendors with your business checks, which should have your business address printed on them.

There are exceptions to the rule of not telling your bank about the business account. If you are a retail operation, for example, establishing a business account with your bank is beneficial because you're dealing with a lot of cash transactions and you'll need to use their business services (acquiring large amounts of change, making daily deposits). Additionally, if you're a retailer, your business will probably have a separate name (Sandra's Treasure Chest; The Bear Necessities) that you'll put on your checks and accounts. But if your business name is your own name, you don't need to clue your bank in. You can even order your checks through your software system.

Your hours of operation

In the last chapter, we talked about the hours during which you would be running your business. We discussed the importance of flexibility in the work you're doing and when you're doing it, which is fine for your own peace of mind. However, in your own mind and in the minds of your clients, you're going to need to set up some kind of standard office hours and stick to them as closely as you possibly can.

In corporate America, you'd work on a weekend if it was required of you, but you'd know you had to be in by 9 and out no earlier than 5. By the same token, that mixture of discipline and flexibility is necessary at home. If nothing else, setting standard work hours—and letting your clients know what those hours are—gives you a starting point and an ending point every day. Being your own boss allows you leniency in both starting and stopping times.

Make It Legal

When you work at home, you no longer have to worry about corporate co-workers, but you do have to worry about a larger entity: the laws of your city and county. In Chapter 4, we'll explore what you'll need to do to keep these factions happy and what's not necessary. We'll also touch upon any credentials you'll need, such as memberships and affiliations, to keep your business legitimate.

◆

Checklist 3 ✎

✓_____ List the essential elements and equipment you'll need to start your business, everything from your desk to your communication needs.

✓_____ Look into equipment and furniture leasing options if you want to reduce your initial capital outlay. Negotiate a buyout option if you can.

✓_____ Do you need equipment-maintenance agreements to save money on repairs?

✓_____ Make friends with your vendors to get the best prices and service.

✓_____ Consider the location of your office/work space and consult with others in the home before making a final decision.

✓_____ Is your work space big enough? Bright enough? Comfortable enough? Quiet enough? Private enough? to allow you to do your work and stop doing your work after business hours?

✓_____ How many phone lines do you realistically need to be efficient? Set up at least three phone lines: one for personal calls (you can add an extension to your home line for this), one for business calls and one for a fax/modem.

✓_____ Shop around for a cost-effective long-distance calling plan, preferably one that earns you frequent-flyer miles or other non-business-related rewards.

✓_____ If you decide to be listed in the phone directory, list your business number under the name of your business rather than under your name.

✓_____ Dedicate a credit card and/or checking account to business transactions (unless you have an accounting software program or an extremely good accountant!).

✓_____ Charge clients a standard 15% markup on outside products and services you use specifically for them.

✓_____ Instead of having mail and deliveries to your home, rent an outside mailbox at a retail mailbox center, rather than the post office.

✓_____ Inform your clients of your business hours.

Notes ✎

Notes ✎

*"Diligence is the
mother of good luck."*
—*Benjamin Franklin*

LEGALLY SPEAKING

4

I n the home-based business person's perfect world, we'd begin our ideal business without worrying about petty little things like licenses, zoning and other credentials. Unfortunately, there are powers-that-be to keep us in line—but then again, they also keep the people with whom we do business in line, so it does balance out in the end. These forces include your city or county's business statutes, the Federal Government and, lest we forget, the Internal Revenue Service.

Naming your business

Once you've decided on the type of business you're going to run (a product-based or service-based operation), the next important decision you'll need to make is what to call it. In some cases, the name of your business will be obvious, particularly if you're buying into an established franchise that will do some of the advertising and marketing for you. In other cases, the choice may not be so simple.

People in service businesses frequently choose to use their own name in titling their company. This can work for many types of HBBs, such as insurance sales or consulting, but I'm not too fond of that idea. If you're well-known in your industry, it might make sense to call your business "Joe Jones Financial Consulting." My feeling is that you need to pick a name for your business that has meaning for you, or that has something to do with type of product you'll offer or work you'll be doing.

Many years ago, I ran a jewelry business that involved visiting homes and corporations, holding "jewelry parties." I would tote 14kt and 18kt gold chains, bracelets, charms and other jewelry accessories with me to the customer's home or to their place of business. People would meet me to make their jewelry purchases. It made sense to call that business Golden Spirit because it fit the essence of that particular venture.

My current public relations and marketing business is called New Directions, a name that I literally dreamed up in the middle of the night. What I like best about that name is that it allows me to move the focus of my business as my business dictates, i.e. moving in New Directions. If I decide to go into advertising, or real estate, or even bridal consulting, the name works for me. It fits a number of diverse sectors and gives me the freedom to change my direction if I need to or if the market so dictates.

Your business name may also evolve from something that's personally significant to you. The name of my publishing company, Stairwell Press, comes from the fact that I run a publishing enterprise from an office on the top floor of my home. The name means something special to me, and it has a nice ring to it for anyone who hears or reads it. How did I arrive at this name? I polled anyone and everyone who was willing to give me feedback (including a number of strangers!), showing them a list of possible names and asking for their favorite three. Stairwell Press won, hands down, so that's the one I chose. I'm not saying that you have to run a nationwide survey to determine your business name, but it certainly doesn't hurt to do some outside market research.

Another example of a great business name is a publication called Book Pages, which is a newsletter magazine that reviews books. This name makes sense for that business, and it's easy for people to remember. My recommendation is to carefully consider what you're going to be doing, and call your business something appropriate to what you're offering. If your business is serious, such as accounting or marriage counseling, don't pick a name that's whimsical. This decision is important. Your company name will be reflected in all your business dealings (stationery, signage, advertising, the phone directory, etc.), and it will be the most prominent representation of what you do.

You may also want to think about an identifying logo for your business. Sometimes a business name will naturally lead to an appropriate logo, as in the case of Stairwell Press. Establishing a business identity via a logo is a major benefit for you, and the adage, "A Picture is Worth a Thousand Words," has never been more valuable. Before you decide for certain to use your own name, consider if a logo will help you in your business.

Once you've decided on your business' name, you'll likely want to register that name by filing a dba (doing business as). Contract your local newspaper to publish an announcement that you are intending to run a business under that name. (Costs for filing a dba vary, depending upon your newspaper). Once you've publicized your statement of intent, you're free to open shop.

A name search is an additional option you may decide to take. Check with the state in which you'll be running your business in order to conduct a name search; again, your local newspaper can give you more information on how to do this. Even if you're using your own name in the business, doing a name search of other businesses in your local area is still not a bad idea and can save you endless headaches. For example, if you decide to call your business Smith Plumbing, and the print shop down the street is called Smith Bros., you may have mail mix-ups and lots of wrong numbers to contend with, which can really be disruptive. A simple name search will solve this problem and alleviate confusion.

Ultimately, the name you elect is a very personal choice that you'll have to live with for a long time, so choose carefully. A few more words to the wise: make sure it's a name the average person can say and spell, and be careful about pigeonholing yourself by choosing a name that defines you too narrowly. You want to allow yourself room to grow and change, especially when you're new to the world of home-based businesses.

Being responsible about business licenses

While we'd often like to close our eyes to the matters of business housekeeping, we need to realize that as an HBB, we're operating in a larger world than just our family and those in our immediate household. The last thing you want is for the city to close you down because your residence is not properly zoned for your business activities. And, if a neighbor complains to the city that clients are coming and going at your house all day long, you'll want to make sure that the city knows about your business well in advance of this situation.

Luckily, with the exponential growth of HBBs, it's becoming easier to get the proper credentials for running your business from home. City, county, state and federal governments are all aware of the proliferation of HBBs and, in some cases, have become much more lenient; even the Internal Revenue Service now allows several tax deductions for HBBs. The bad news is that some laws do tax the HBB businessperson for the privilege of running his or her home business. This is where you can run into potentially sticky situations should you choose to ignore the law.

Though in some cases, you might consider keeping quiet about such matters, the belief that honesty is always the best policy, works in your favor here. First, find out what your city's restrictions are for HBBs. If you want to hedge your bets, call the business license bureau or the licensing department of your city anonymously and tell them you're thinking about working from home. Each city has a different name for the agency that issues business licenses, so query them about that agency. Find out what the legal ramifications are for the kind of business you're planning, and they'll refer you to the appropriate party. Of course, once you find out what's required, you can choose to ignore it, but be aware that if you get caught, you could pay a hefty penalty.

More often than not, if you're in a service-type business where no one comes to your home (i.e. writers, bookkeepers), you'll be charged a flat rate for a business license. Unless you have employees, this should suffice. For the purposes of this discussion, let's say that you don't have to deal with employees or worker's compensation. The standard license rate should apply in almost all of these cases.

Case Study

NAME: Dan Poynter
NAME OF BUSINESS: Para Publishing
TYPE OF BUSINESS: Nonfiction book publisher, also provides resources for those writing and publishing their own books.
ESTABLISHED: 1968
OCCUPATION BEFORE BECOMING HOME-BASED: Parachute Designer.
REASON FOR BECOMING HOME-BASED: Wrote a book on designing parachutes. He needed to publish the book and decided to do it himself. One major reason for self-publishing of his first book was that he knew who to target for book sales.

The short commute is the best benefit from Dan's home-based business. He also praises the low start-up costs and the ability to "ease into it." To effectively run his business, he only needs phone lines and access to the post office.

Dan has seen many potential pitfalls. His most important advice falls into legal categories. First, know what you can deduct from your house. He advises you to "draw a plan of your house and determine which percentage of each room is used for your business." For instance, the bedroom is not used at all, while the office is used 100%. He conducts meetings and workshops in his house, so he is also able to deduct portions of his living room and kitchen (food preparation). Altogether, he deducts more than 50% of his housing expenses. This sounds like a high number, but in Dan's case it is realistic. Get the advice of a tax attorney after you draw up you plans and determine your deductions.

A second bit of legal advice is to promptly get your business license and tax resale certificates (if needed). A good rule is to always think about taxes ahead of time and avoid potential losses. He even advises that you include tax ramifications for your business in your will or trust so that your heirs do not suffer from unexpected tax surprises.

Taking the next steps

Once you've gone to the city and discussed what restrictions might apply to your business, you may need to contact the state. (The city should be able to refer you to a state agency, as well.) If you're doing business out-of-state, there may be legal issues that need to be addressed. For example, if your business involves shipping gourmet food, you should be aware of the restriction around sending alcohol outside state lines. You might need a special permit. It's important to investigate whatever restrictions might apply for whatever business you're conducting.

In addition, it's not a bad idea to get a Sales Tax Resale license. This allows you to purchase products on behalf of your clients at wholesale prices. If you resell these products to your clients, you must charge them appropriate sales tax (unless they have given you their Sales Tax Resale number). There are many ways that a Sales Tax Resale license can work to your advantage. For example, if you are creating a sales package for your client, the vendor you are working with will likely charge you tax. But if you have a Sales Tax Resale number, you can forego paying the tax, passing it along to the end user—your client—along with a markup for the service that you negotiated at wholesale. Be aware, however, that at year's end, you are responsible to your State Board of Equalization for the sales taxes that you've charged and received. Your bookkeeper or tax accountant will explain this procedure more specifically to your business.

When you negotiate with vendors, let them know you have a resale number. Hopefully, you'll be paying a wholesale or "professional" price and will be able to add your markup. It's another way to add to your income. Naturally, you have to report to the IRS whatever tax you charge on items you resell to your clients.

In my business, I deal in paper goods, so I negotiate with paper houses to buy pocket folders, envelopes and other paper items at wholesale prices. I show my clients what I've purchased and I add a markup to that price and charge them sales tax. I'm reselling these items to my clients, so I get a different price than what "Joe Public" walking in off the street pays. It's a win/win situation, even though it's a little bit of paperwork for me. But remember that you can negotiate better pricing as a wholesaler than at the retail level.

Each month, I do a recount of those items I've sold to my clients for which I've charged a markup. I have a dollar volume of what I've purchased outside, what my markup has been and what sales tax has been received. When I pay the State Board of Equalization (which you may have to do quarterly), I pay back the sales tax I've collected. By keeping accurate monthly records, it's easy for me to stay on top of the issue.

It's also important to note here that some clients may be out-of-state. Be aware of the sales tax charged in those areas, for end-of-the-year reporting. Though you purchase products for use in your own state, and charge your clients the going state sales tax rate, your bookkeeper or accountant will have to figure out-of-state sales tax at the end of the year, and report it accordingly. In some instances, you are required to charge the sales tax rate for the other state—the one to which you are shipping your product out-of-state.

Specific credentials and memberships

Depending upon what type of business you're running, you may need additional certification. If you're an insurance agent, for instance, you may need a special insurance certificate from the agency that governs that profession. You also should keep up with the same professional memberships you would have if you were working for a corporate entity outside your home. I belong to the Association for Women in Communication (AWC) because it keeps me in touch with other women whose job requirements are similar. You might choose to belong to the Chamber of Commerce as a way of networking and legitimizing your business.

There may be licenses that will help you expand your business. I'm registered with the City of Redondo Beach in California, and I get notifications on events taking place that could be beneficial to expand my business. If I didn't have the license, I wouldn't know about these events and could miss an opportunity to profit. This license is a mere $99 a year, which is really arbitrary, and yet the association is quite beneficial to me.

It's important to research what the licensing factors will be for your business, and to figure that into your operating costs. Remember that these costs are tax deductible.

Other restrictions

Suppose you have been a skin-care specialist for 25 years and want to set up a skin-care business in your home. You decide that it's much more conducive to a stress-free skin-care treatment for your customers to come to your home than to go to a retail environment or an office building. People visit your home regularly for facials and other treatments, and the neighbors begin to complain because visiting clients are creating tremendous parking problems. You could be put out of business by the city because you're not zoned to run that kind of business from your home.

However, if you've gone to the city and made a case for your business, and the city says you can't, at least you've tried. It may be more difficult for them to close you down, or they may decide to change the zoning laws in your area if enough HBBs are complaining about the laws.

You may wonder if running this type of business from your home takes away from the legitimacy of it. My initial response to this is that it depends on your attitude. If you're serious about your business, chances are your customers will take you seriously, as well. You might be able to reduce your fees because your overhead is lower at home than in a retail establishment. Be aware, too, that getting a business license and hanging it on the wall of your treatment room will help bolster your own—and others'—perception of your business. After all, you are paying income taxes and license fees on it, which also helps establish your business with your accountant at year's end.

To incorporate or not to incorporate: That is the question.

I am a sole proprietor doing business as New Directions, even though I never filed New Directions formally with the state of California. It may sound illegal, but it isn't. The only reason to file is to help protect the name of your business. Have a discussion with your accountant and your attorney as whether or not filing a business name is a necessity for you and your business.

Incorporation is another matter—a relatively expensive one. It's also not usually necessary for most HBBs. The only reason to incorporate is to protect yourself from legal liability after the fact. You don't have to incorporate if you write your contracts to protect yourself. You may still be sued personally, but incorporating protects you from personal liability. When you deal with clients, make sure that both the client company and its principals are specified in the contract. Know who it is you're dealing with and who, ultimately, will be responsible for paying you for your services.

On tax I.D. numbers

When you incorporate, you get a corporate tax I.D. number. If you don't incorporate, your tax I.D. number is your Social Security number. Should you fall into this category (as most HBBs do), when clients fill out their 1099 forms at the end of the year, they should file your name—not your business name—because the IRS may not recognize your business name. For these matters, your attorney and your accountant are more important than in any other situation. While it may be tempting to have your brother-in-law, who does your personal income taxes, handle your business income taxes, I strongly recommend getting a good business accountant to whom you're not related. Get yourself an accountant and/or tax person who understands your business and the way it operates, and has experience with HBBs. It could be the smartest investment you make for your business—and your peace of mind.

Be thorough

It's a good idea to do all the necessary research on business licenses and credentials before you start your business, so that you know from the start what you can and can not do. A few well-placed phone calls early on can save you a lot of time, money and aggravation down the road.

Show me the money!

In the next chapter, we'll explore the financial aspects of running an HBB, including paying yourself a salary, insurance coverage, paying employees and figuring out if you're really making a profit on your newfound venture.

Checklist 4 ✎

✓———— Call the business license bureau or licensing department and find out your city's restrictions for home-based businesses, including zoning laws and customer parking restrictions (if applicable).

✓———— Choose a name for your business that reflects the professionality you need for success.

✓———— Apply for a business license, if one is necessary. Post it where clients and customers can see it clearly.

✓———— With an attorney, explore any legal ramifications of running your business.

✓———— If you purchase products for which you charge your clients, get a tax resale license to allow you to pay wholesale prices. Pay the State Board of Equalization the sales tax you've collected from your clients. (Be aware of out-of-state sales taxes, and report them accordingly.)

✓———— Stay up-to-date on any certifications or credentials required to run your business.

✓———— Join agencies and organizations that will help you expand your business and social contacts.

✓———— With your accountant and attorney, discuss the pros and cons of incorporating your business. For most home-based businesses, incorporating is unnecessary.

✓———— If you don't incorporate, remind your clients to use your name, not your business' name, when filling out their 1099 tax forms at year end.

✓———— Make sure your accountant/tax preparer is a professional who is familiar with your business, how it works and what you do.

Notes

Notes ✎

"Money never starts an idea;
it is the idea that
starts the money."
　　　　　　—*W.J. Cameron*

FINANCES

5

There are two essential ingredients necessary to successfully manage the financial aspects of running a business from home: capital and discipline. If you start out with sufficient capital and maintain a disciplined system for managing it, you'll be able to sleep easier at night and you'll be less likely to panic when life throws you curves (and we all know that it will).

Have enough for a rainy day?

One of the most important things you can do when starting an HBB is to have enough money in the bank to cover your living expenses during the initial stages. How much is enough? Aim for at least enough to see you through the first three to six months, even if you don't make a dime. Like any other start-up, the beginning stages raise income questions—who will pay me and when, how much should I charge for my product or service? What time frame shall I give my clients to pay the bill? If you're selling a product, your cash flow depends upon how much you sell. In a service business, whether you charge for specific projects, or go on a monthly retainer, your cash flow is most likely to be a little unsteady and uneven at first. Couple that with high out-of-pocket expenses, and you're likely to feel a bit panicked. After all, you do need to eat and keep a roof over your head. It's essential, therefore, to establish some sort of financial cushion before you go out on your own. It's important, too, to replace whatever you take from your cushion as soon as you can so that you don't drain your resources. Think of the cushion as a bank that you can borrow from and pay back without disturbing other sources of household income.

When I started my business, I was able to refinance a small piece of property that I'd owned forever. By doing that, I cushioned myself financially so that I could work my business without any sort of income, if necessary. The cushion provided me with what I needed to get by, and living frugally allowed me to invest into a high-yield money-market account. That money has been a godsend for me and over the years, I've had numerous unexpected expenses paid for from that account. And yes, it's very important to pay it back—that's where discipline counts the most.

Case Study

NAME: Kevin Nunley
NAME OF BUSINESS: Kevin Nunley Associates
TYPE OF BUSINESS: Marketing advice and copy writing
ESTABLISHED: On the Internet since 1996
OCCUPATION BEFORE BECOMING HOME-BASED:
21 years in radio and TV, both on-air and in management
REASON FOR BECOMING HOME-BASED:
"To be my own boss and spend more time with family."

Knowing you have a steady flow of customers can help ease your financial worries. Kevin started his business before leaving his full-time position, and at first, was getting almost no customers. He soon realized that he had to leave his job in order to devote his energies to his home-based business.

"From the first day I went at it full-time, business suddenly began to pour in and it hasn't stopped," he says. "But initially, the greatest obstacle I encountered was getting enough business to turn my 'hobby' into a steady-earning business."

Kevin chose to use technology to his advantage, flooding the Internet with articles he'd written that other business people would find helpful. "I'm not a great writer, so I kept the words simple and sentences short. It's hard to go wrong when you keep things simple. I got books from the library and used other authors' ideas to inspire my own writing."

His system worked, and before long, business began to flow with people treating him like a big-name expert. In fact, business is growing at such a rate that one of Kevin's future challenges and goals is to keep up with customer demand without sacrificing low price or quality.

"I strongly recommend the same strategy to everyone," says Kevin. "If you don't like to write, get editing help from a pro, your kid's English teacher, your cousin the journalism student or your spouse."

On another note, Kevin addresses the isolation many people feel when they begin working at home. "It's easy to feel like a fish out of water when you actually speak to someone face-to-face. You also find yourself overdoing it when you converse with the woman at the grocery checkout stand, simply because she may be the only human you've seen all day."

Where to get the money

Of course, managing your money and actually having the money to invest in a new business are two very different things. For many new HBB entrepreneurs, raising capital is a chief concern. If you don't happen to have any inheritances handy, your first stop may be as simple as your local bank. Unfortunately, many banks are still unwilling to lend capital for small, start-up operations (home-based or otherwise) because they see these ventures as too risky. This is where you need to get creative.

A good source for home-based business loans is the Small Business Administration (SBA). According to an article in the May '99 issue of Gifts & Decorative Accessories, a trade publication for the gift industry, the SBA's guaranteed loan program has recently become even more appealing to small business owners. SBA guarantees repayment of the loan to a bank for an interest fee. Advantages include favorable terms of repayment, qualification of more than 90% of all U.S. businesses and low financing costs. Shop around for a bank with experience in SBA lending for the best loan arrangement.

Another thing you can do to raise capital is look for investors. According to the article "Secrets of Successfully Starting Your Own Business," available on the Small Business Resource Center (SBRC) website, this requires putting together a business plan or prospectus, knowing how much money you want, exactly how it will be used and how you intend to repay it. Then you'll need to spread the word to potential investors, either through advertising or creating an investment group of your peers. You might also consider approaching small-business investment companies in your local area; you can look them up in the phone book under Investment Services. The SBRC says these companies "exist for the sole purpose of lending money to businesses which they feel have a good chance of becoming successful. In many instances, they trade their help for a small interest in your company."

Another SBRC recommendation is to approach your state Business Development Commission, which can offer favorable taxes, business expertise and the money or facilities to help a new business get started. Check your Chamber of Commerce for more information.

Other options for raising capital include industrial banks, insurance companies and money brokers. With the burgeoning numbers of home-based entrepreneurs in this country, the lending market is bound to begin offering more options to small business owners. Do a little research on the subject, either on the Internet or at your local library, and you'll find a wealth of information available to you.

Case Study

NAME: Arthur Vanick
NAME OF BUSINESS: The Digital Voice/Picture This Video
TYPE OF BUSINESS: Audio/video production
ESTABLISHED: 1989
ESTIMATED ANNUAL INCOME OF BUSINESS: $5,000 to $30,000
OCCUPATION BEFORE BECOMING HOME-BASED:
Group leader in classified area at TRW
REASON FOR BECOMING HOME-BASED: "Additional income."

Arthur has his fingers into many different pies. In addition to running his home-based audio/video company, he owns an apartment building that nets him an income of $50,000 per year, and he does voice-overs for entertainment media.

His advice to anyone starting out in a home-based business is, "Always treat customers with respect and do every job as if it were for yourself. Always charge what the job is worth, get a written contract with an advance deposit, and don't give "deals" because they usually backfire on you."

Arthur believes in giving 100% of himself to any project he does, which pays off in long-term, loyal customers and clients. "I'm still in occasional contact with a couple whose wedding video we did several years ago," he shares. "They still like the video so much that they play it many times every month."

In the future, Arthur says he would like to expand into the digital realm and increase computer involvement in the production end of his business. He feels fortunate to be able to participate in so many arenas he loves—a definite perk of being in charge of your own time.

"On the audio end of things, it looks like my voice may soon be featured in an animated movie that is currently in production," he says. "And toward the end of 1998, I garnered my first voice-over credit in a comedy/science fiction movie."

You mean I'm supposed to pay myself a salary?

The issue of your salary is less complex than it may seem. It is my opinion that there are few absolutes when it comes to salary, provided you keep good records. Let's look at what usually happens when you start an HBB. Since most individual HBBs are not incorporated (the reasons for this were explained in Chapter 4), it is likely that entrepreneurs commingle funds with other household members in order to pay living expenses. This is not necessarily a bad practice because you have the freedom to move money around as you need to. But if you're smart, you'll have hired an accountant or bookkeeper to sort it all out at the back end—before tax time.

If you have a spouse, you might consider keeping your accounts separate—i.e, do not commingle your funds. Keep a separate business account and use some of it to help pay for certain living expenses. In this case, whatever monies you use to that end becomes your salary. This may not work initially because your expenses may exceed your income for awhile. (Here's where that financial cushion becomes really useful!)

Whichever system you use, it's important to communicate with the other financial contributors of the household and establish what portion of the living expenses will be your responsibility.

Personally, I don't pay myself a salary. All of my bills are paid out of a single checking account. How do I keep it all straight? I maintain good records, utilizing a user-friendly software program to tag all my income and expenses. There are several excellent software programs on the market today, some even targeting small businesses such as Quicken or Quickbooks, that help you keep your records in good order. Talk to your bookkeeper or accountant about which program is best for your needs; it will help make their life much easier! Or ask the computer store sales associate, who is likely to be more up-to-date about programs.

You'll need to allocate monies for your own personal needs (not household expenses), as well. Based on your income, this figure may fluctuate from month to month, so it's important to determine a minimal base. Be realistic about budgeting for personal expenses that are essential to your self-esteem and well-being. Perhaps it's a manicure, a clothing allowance or your gym membership. Whatever it may be, be sure to include that tiny luxury!

The key to the salary issue is accurate record keeping. If your HBB is your only source of income, then it's easier not to pay yourself a salary. But being prudent about your financials is also really important. When you do have a good month, set aside at least half of the overage in a savings account. Remember your mother's advice about saving for a rainy day? Those words have never been more important.

Time to do the billing!

When you worked outside the home for someone else, you probably barely thought about how or when you were going to get paid. Someone in human resources or the accounting department or perhaps the boss him/herself paid you regularly. But when you're working from home—either for someone else or in a home-based business—you need to think about your income and its timing quite frequently.

If you work from home for a corporation, you've probably already established that you'll be receiving a weekly or bimonthly paycheck. It's usually not an issue, unless you are an independent contractor for that corporation, in which case you are expected to produce an invoice for your services. In a home-based business, billing is quite another story.

If you're selling a product, it's pretty much a moot point. Most likely, you have a cash-and-carry situation where you get paid at the time you sell the product. You've determined what the price will be in advance, taking into account your production and labor costs, overhead, materials, packaging and any other expenses, so that you're making a profit at the end of the month.

A service-oriented home-based business is run quite differently. One of the biggest problems that home-based service-oriented businesses run into is not establishing the parameters of payment before starting the job. Perhaps your client is expecting to pay you 30 days after you finish the job because you haven't communicated to him that you need money up front for expenses. This kind of miscommunication can create conflict that can cost you business, so it's vitally important that you make the conditions of your payment clearly understood early on.

That said, there are a number of ways to bill a service-oriented business: by retainer, by the hour, by the project, or by the outcome. In a retainer-based business, the client pays you a set fee for a specific period of time worked—usually monthly. You may put in 50 hours one month and 10 the next, but the retainer remains the same. You send the client an invoice every month for your retainer and any agreed-upon out-of-pocket expenses.

In an hourly-rate business, you charge by the hour and are expected to keep clear records of the amount of time you spend working for each client. That means if you call your Aunt Martha and talk to her for 30 minutes in the middle of working for XYZ Company, you don't bill the company for that time. There's an honor system at work here, and you'd be wise to adhere to it, but don't sell yourself short either. If you reviewed your work one last time while the 11:00 news was on in the background, you still get to bill for that time. You may need to indicate to your client in advance roughly how many hours you anticipate spending on a project, or agree to a ceiling in order to keep the client's costs down. If you're doing the work in the client's office, hourly billing is usually not called into question, but you still need to be very diligent about keeping track of the hours you work.

Project-based businesses are quite common because both you and the client know in advance exactly how high the bill will be. One drawback to project-based businesses is that you probably can't bill extra for additional unforeseen work, and there may not be a specified time limit. In this scenario, a project could drag on for months before you get paid. A smart way to bill project-based businesses with long deadlines is to bill a percentage up front (say, 30% of your estimated total bill) another third halfway into the project, and the final third upon completion. This way, both you and your client experience fair compensation. Also, you may want to stipulate clearly in your contract or letter of agreement (another must!) exactly what you'll do for that fee, indicating that work outside those parameters will cost the client more.

Finally, outcome-based business pays according to the results of your work, usually in the form of a commission or bonus based on, for example, the number of solid leads received from an ad you placed or the number of clips generated from a press release you distributed. Outcome-based billing is usually done in addition to another form of billing, whether retainer, project-based or hourly.

However you choose to bill, one fact is immutable: you must do your billing in a timely and regular manner, with scrupulous follow-up. You do that by making sure you get paid and making that a priority. If you don't, you'll go out of business before you know it because you'll run out of operating capital. Cash flow is essential when you're in a home-based business.

You can't expect your clients to pay you unless they are billed, so be sure to keep clear and thorough records of your charges for each client, and send out your invoices consistently, either at the end of the month, the beginning of the month or the end of a project. Set aside a time to do it like clockwork, and your cash flow will be much smoother.

I also highly advise you to put a time frame for payment on your invoices. Usually anywhere from two weeks to 30 days is advisable. The good news is this age of technology, which allows us the opportunity to work at home, also provides us with programs that will not only put due dates on our invoices, but help us keep track of our billing. There are some wonderful user friendly software programs (Quicken, QuickBooks and MicroSoft Works make several) that will date and format your invoices, as well as keep track of who owes you money, how much they owe and how much you owe. Few people like to ask for money, much less talk about it, but just as you want to take care of your clients so that they will continue to utilize your services, you must also take care of yourself. Sometimes we need to put our clients' ethics in check and keep them on track.

You may also have some concerns about pricing your services. I won't go into detail about how much to charge for your particular business because there are too many individual factors to take into account. I would suggest you do your research: talk to other people in your industry and get a feel for what clients are willing to pay for what you're selling. Read books about doing business independently in your field. Decide how much your time, effort and expertise are worth. You may be able to give clients a break because you don't have the overhead of an outside office. However, you don't want to underbid yourself so that you're resentful over not being paid what you're worth; similarly, you don't want to price yourself out of your market simply because you can charge whatever you like.

Make deductions easier

One of the perks of keeping good records is that your accountant can find deductions that might not have been clear without thorough financial data. For example, I have a housekeeper, and because my office is part of my house, a portion of her fee can be deducted as a business expense, much like an office cleaning service would be part of office maintenance. Though her fee is paid from the one account, the percentages are noted and are assigned a separate accounting number. When I pull up the physical expenses of my business on my computer, I know that 20% of my housekeeper's fee has been designated as a business expense. By the same token, you have rent or a mortgage, electricity and telephone bills, plus vendors and other outside services that may be applicable as business expenses.

If you're keeping good records, it's a smart idea to do a quarterly overview of your expenses vs. income. I retain an outside bookkeeper who helps me balance my books and pulls up questions about monetary assignments. The good news about that is I can then judge much more specifically what I need to do in order to keep myself afloat and comfortable—whether to push for more business or to cut back because I'm overwhelmed.

Insurance: Protecting yourself from liability and other catastrophes

If you've worked for someone else in the past, they probably had group coverage health insurance. In some cases, if you're within the 18-month COBRA limit, you can still get health insurance coverage from your previous employer. (COBRA refers to group health-insurance coverage for which you pay the premiums; your employer is required by law to offer you this coverage for up to 18 months after you leave your job.) Before you do that, though, shop around for a policy that meets your needs at a reasonable price. More and more insurance companies are providing suitable policies for HBB entrepreneurs. Also, recognize that your health insurance needs may have changed: you're no longer around as many people so the likelihood of contracting the flu has diminished. You might be better off taking a policy with lower premiums and higher deductibles. Whatever you do, don't go without any health insurance—you wouldn't drive a car without auto insurance, would you?

Life or term insurance is another consideration. Term insurance tends to be less expensive, and might be a particularly good idea if you have property and/or equipment. If you have any sort of financial obligations that will fall on someone else in the event of your death, a life-insurance policy will help them deal with those obligations.

Liability and equipment insurance are of utmost importance. Keep in mind that you may already have this coverage on your renter's or homeowner's insurance policy, but it's wise to check with your insurance company to be safe. You may need business insurance, either liability to protect you if someone should hurt themselves in your office, or insurance on your equipment in case your fax machine starts a house fire. Be aware that most homeowner's policies don't cover business equipment for theft or fire. The best course of action is to talk to your insurance agent to determine your needs and subsequent coverage.

Depending on your business, you may need liability insurance that protects you from being sued by a client who claims you responsible for negligence or damages. Your client contract should specifically limit any legal liabilities for which you may be responsible. Of course, it's always a good idea to have your contract legally reviewed prior to its use, just to be on the safe side. We'd all like to think that the client relationship is built on trust and goodwill, but unfortunately, in today's environment, it's not necessarily the case.

The good news is most liability and business-equipment policies are very reasonably priced, probably just $10 or $15 a month. Don't be penny-wise and dollar-foolish about a business expense that can be deducted as a cost of doing business.

On the other hand, don't overstep your bounds on tax deductions by, for example, taking friends out to dinner all the time because you can write it off. These may be just the kinds of red flags that will tip off the IRS and trigger an audit of your business. Be smart about tax deductions, but don't take unnecessary risks.

Subcontractors vs. employees: Which works better for you?

There are both financial and practical advantages to choosing subcontractors over employees. When you hire subcontractors, you don't take taxes out of their wages, and you are not liable for their insurance needs. However, the liability factor goes up with the number of people you have coming into your office—that's where liability insurance is really important.

When you talk to the state or county about registering a business license (see Chapter 4), or when you talk to your insurance agent, ask if there's an insurance requirement for employees. Also, find out about your worker's compensation responsibilities.

Depending on the volume of your business and your time requirements, most HBB entrepreneurs can keep themselves afloat by using subcontractors. With regard to income taxes, you can pay someone up to $600 a year without being required to issue a 1099 form. Discuss this situation with your accountant—he or she can tell you whether it makes more sense to hire an outside service or bring someone in.

My feeling is, if you're small enough to run your business out of your home, you probably don't need employees. I know a manufacturing facility in upstate New York that has 35 to 40 workers at any given time, the majority of whom are subcontractors. This enables the company to circumvent the tax responsibility and bookkeeping requirements that come with hiring employees.

111

Here in Southern California, the aerospace industry has frequently relied on "permanent temporary" employment agencies to provide workers and pay their salaries and benefits. The initial outlay for the hiring company is higher, but the liability and tax consequences are lower.

The independent contractors have to pay their own taxes, but they receive higher wages up front and they have the flexibility to work the hours they want.

Because my work ebbs and flows, part-time, subcontract or piece-meal work operates best for me. When my cash flow is low, I can choose to do the legwork myself and save a little money. The choice is yours, dependent on the workings of your business.

Are you really making a profit?

The numbers don't lie, but they can certainly be manipulated. It reminds me of the story of the woman who kept overdrawing her checking account. Because she still had unused checks in her checkbook, she reasoned she still had money left in her account. If you utilize the services of a quarterly, if not monthly, bookkeeper you should be able to tell if you're in the black or in the red. If you're organized and have kept accurate records, you'll be able to go back through them and say either, "Wow! I really have made a profit," or "Here's where I can cut back." Of course, if your tax bill keeps going up each year, you know you're making a profit, even if it doesn't feel like it!

Rather than focusing on how much money you're making, remember why you got into this business in the first place. Hard work and frugality are key to making an HBB work. Being in an HBB is not about getting rich. It's about being comfortable. It's about living your life the way you want to live it. It's about working smarter, not harder. If you get rich, fabulous! If you're an inventor and you invent something that everybody needs and wants, more power to you! Ultimately, being in an HBB is about working the business, not letting the business work you. That's more important to your self-esteem than any dollar figure.

Along the way...

Once you get your HBB off the ground, you may run into some roadblocks. Loneliness, disorganization and poor spending choices are some common problems. In the next chapter, we'll discuss how to recognize, avoid and transcend these roadblocks so that your HBB can continue to thrive.

Checklist 5 ✎

✓_____ Have you accumulated enough capital to see you through 3-6 months, even if you don't make a dime of profit? If you dip into your cushion, pay yourself back as soon as you can.

✓_____ Consider that paying yourself a salary may be unnecessary if you keep thorough and accurate records.

✓_____ Be reasonable about your living expenses: be neither extravagant nor miserly.

✓_____ With your accountant, explore all possible tax deductions you might reap from working at home.

✓_____ Do a quarterly overview of expenses vs. income.

✓_____ Shop around for a good health insurance policy that covers you and your dependents adequately.

✓_____ Consider your life insurance needs and build premiums into your budget if necessary.

✓_____ Think about liability and equipment insurance needs. Research companies to find the best rates.

✓_____ Opt for subcontractors over employees if you can.

✓_____ Utilize the services of a good bookkeeper to determine whether you're making a profit or dipping into the red.

✓_____ Remember that running a home-based business is about working the business, not letting the business work you.

Notes 🖉

"If the only tool you have is a hammer, you tend to see every problem as a nail."
—*Abraham H. Maslow*

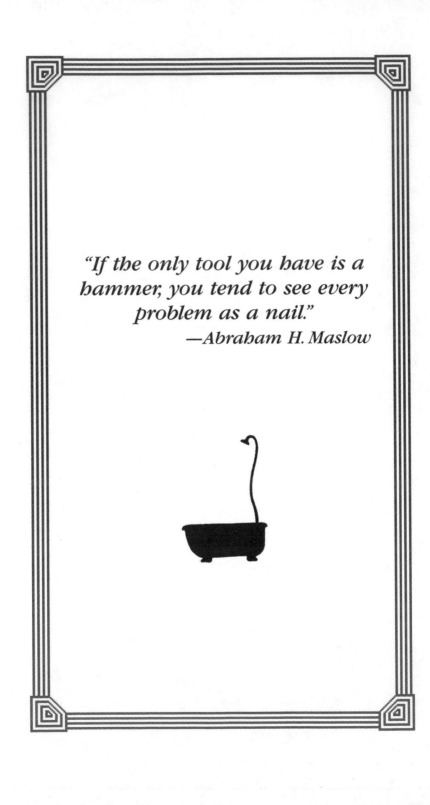

THE TRICKS OF THE TRADE

6

Staying organized and disciplined among the chaos

A long time ago, a friend offered me a pearl of wisdom. I'd like to share it with you: When you're faced with 600 things coming at you, all at the same time—things like: you've got three deadlines, a photo shoot in an hour and you haven't gotten props, the IRS is knockin' at your door, and your son wants you to go to the Open House that night but you need to work—think about eating an elephant.

"An elephant?" you say? Yes, an elephant! When you look at an elephant, it seems an enormous animal—how would you ever eat an entire elephant? Well, there's only one way: one bite at a time! The thought of handling everything you're faced with is overwhelming, right? But, if you take it one bite at a time, eventually everything gets done.

Try this little experiment. Take a sheet of paper, shred it into strips, wad up those strips and throw them up in the air, all at once. Now, try to follow each of them as they make their way down. What happened? You never got a clear picture of any one wad making it to the floor, right? Now, try it again, only this time focus on one wad all the way down. I'll bet you were able to see all the others, or at least most of them, in your peripheral vision.

The point of this little experiment is: if you focus on one project—usually the most important or urgent one—the others will automatically assume an order of priority. Concentrate on one task that has to be accomplished right now, one that you know you can accomplish or that requires immediate attention. You'll be surprised at how stabilizing it can be to focus on one thing, knowing that all of the other things need to be done anyway. Simply by finishing one project, completing the cycle of action, you have a real sense of accomplishment and can move on to the others in a timely fashion.

This is not to say that we can't be multi-tasking. Some of us have a real ability to do many things at once. For example, I can organize my desk and have a business conversation at the same time. However, I may not be able to add word processing to the mix and do all three at the same time. Everyone has limits to how many responsibilities can be juggled in a single period of time. Know your own limits.

Case Study

NAME/BUSINESS NAME: Janice Blair
TYPE OF BUSINESS: Graphics Arts, Illustration, and Calligraphy
ESTABLISHED: 1975
OCCUPATION BEFORE BECOMING HOME-BASED:
Elementary-school teacher

REASON FOR BECOMING HOME-BASED: Desire to trade the task of "taming 35 energetic young students" for the "flexibility, quiet, and comforts of working at home."

More than two decades ago, Janice "casually decided to quit" her teaching job. As she puts it, " I didn't know what I wanted to do, but reasoned that I had my little VW Bug, my Pentax camera; a nice apartment and my resourceful self!" The key to her success was her determination to stay flexible and watch for opportunities to fill special niches. Today, Janice advises those new to a home-based business that "when you offer something unique, you will have all the business that you want." Do not limit yourself, but stay flexible in your work as you strive to fill that special niche. Janice also advises you to "listen carefully to what your clients say AND what they don't say."

An unintended benefit of working from home occurred when Janice began raising her family. She had the luxury of staying home while her children were growing up. She arranged her working hours so that she could participate in their activities and lives.

Janice's future goals involve projects around her house and in her studio. Now that she has converted many files to her computer, she needs to clean her studio of old files to increase efficiency. She also plans to spend more time on painting for personal pleasure and tackle some unfinished home projects.

The ubiquitous Things-To-Do list

I have to confess that I'm not the best person in the world at making and adhering to Things-To-Do lists, but there are times when I do find them helpful. When I do take the time to write a TTD list, and I'm able to visualize what needs to be done and assign a potential time bite to the project, I can then juggle between the little less important projects and the larger, more consequential projects, so that at the end of the day, I feel like I've accomplished something. Tools, like lists, can help you feel productive, which is the key to keeping yourself organized and not feeling overwhelmed.

One caveat about lists: you don't want to make little notes to yourself all day long and end up with dozens of TTD lists. Be organized and disciplined about list-making, or you'll ultimately defeat the whole purpose of this practice.

Managing your time

A colleague of mine who was the managing editor of a major magazine for many years told me about a conversation she once had with her boss. Feeling overwhelmed and noting my friend's ability to handle many different tasks in a time-efficient manner, her boss asked her what her secret was. Here's what she said: "When I have many things to accomplish in a short period of time, I list them all. I quickly find myself doing the things that only take a few minutes because I can cross them off my list, making it more manageable. I've soon whittled my list down to a few major projects that each require a sizeable chunk of time, and I pick the most urgent, taking it as far as I can that day. Then I start on the next big project and take that to the limit. I continue in this manner until everything's crossed off my list. When I tackle things systematically, I rarely feel overwhelmed."

There are a number of tricks you can use to make your use of time more efficient. Here are a few of them.

⧗ Designate a certain amount of time to a particular project. Stop working on it after the time is up and move on to something else.

⧗ Maximize your time out of the office. If you're picking up the mail, pick up your cleaning at the same time.

⏳ Utilize the "multi-story house" principle: when you leave a room, try to bring something with you that needs to go to another part of the house. This way, you'll cut down on the number of trips you make from room to room or floor to floor.

⏳ Work on what has to be done first today, and tackle tomorrow's projects tomorrow. This sounds overly simplistic, but you'd be surprised how many people waste time worrying about projects that are due way in the future, and ignore projects that have to be finished right away.

Whatever system you use, make sure it's one you're comfortable with. For example, there may be certain times of the day or week when you're more adept at handling certain projects. Some projects, like prospecting, follow-up calls or ordering supplies, must be done during business hours, while others, like filing, opening mail, any kind of writing, are more easily accomplished before or after business hours, when you're least likely to be interrupted. If you're more creative in the evening, handle your strategizing or writing projects then. If you tend to wind down at the end of the day, do mindless work like collating and envelope stuffing. Pay attention to your body clock, and you'll be a lot more productive.

Also pay attention to what you enjoy. I love looking through magazines and finding my clients have been mentioned, so I'll tackle this task whenever I'm feeling frustrated. This way, I don't feel depressed at having to do something I don't like when I'm not feeling my best.

Case Study

NAME: Amy Stavis, publisher
NAME OF BUSINESS: Tableware Today
TYPE OF BUSINESS: Trade publication for the tabletop industry
ESTABLISHED: 1993
ESTIMATED ANNUAL INCOME OF BUSINESS: Well over six figures
OCCUPATION BEFORE BECOMING HOME-BASED:
Editor for a trade magazine—and before that, a teacher
REASON FOR BECOMING HOME-BASED:
"Being home with my daughter."

The energetic mother of a six-year-old girl and head of a successful magazine, Amy says she loves working out of her home and feels completely comfortable having her business and personal lives meld together. The one negative she's found is finding the discipline not to put in too many overtime hours.

"I'm working a lot more than I did before I was home-based," Amy admits. "That's because it's right here, and I don't really consider it work because I love it so much. On the other hand, I have the luxury of saying I want to work now and not later. I'm home when the repairmen come, and my hours are totally mine."

She warns of the need to be disciplined and stay focused on work, even though you're home. "There's the feeling that you're playing hooky, that you're not where you're supposed to be because you don't go outside the home to an office. That could be dangerous to some people."

Amy comments that many of her clients have become personal friends, and having her daughter's voice in the background has not heeded her business any, since she approaches it with a sense of humor. In fact, her daughter's bathroom is across the hall from Amy's office, and rather than being distracting, Amy finds this a positive influence and time saver.

"I get to sit at my computer and work for 45 extra minutes while my daughter is taking a bath. After she finishes eating lunch, we run out to get the mail."

Amy has enjoyed wearing all the hats of a home-based business person since she admittedly has a hands-on personality.

"When you have your own business, you do everything in your company. I know the post people and I take every phone call that comes in. I like that aspect of it."

One of her future goals is to become technologically proficient. Amy doesn't have Internet access or e-mail because she feels she spends too much time on the computer as it is and prefers telephone or face-to-face contact. However, as more and more of her clients have developed websites, she feels the pull of the Information Age upon her and knows she will soon succumb to it.

Get up and get out

Sometimes, when the going gets rough and I just can't take it anymore, I literally get up and leave the scene. When you're overwhelmed, often what you really need is a breather, a time-out, as it were. That's the time I go to the department store that's having a sale or do my grocery shopping or have lunch with a friend or go to the movies. Or sometimes it's just a good excuse to walk the dog around the block and try to clear my head of all the pressure.

Other times, I just pace! I call a friend and listen to them for awhile and make plans for the weekend, pacing all the while, or I'll even jump on the treadmill for 15 minutes (that's really pacing!) to quell anxiety or nervous energy. Obviously, the work doesn't vanish when you do. But when you come back, you have a different perspective, and you may even come up with a great idea while you're on that treadmill!

Believe it or not, watching mindless TV (soap operas, talk shows, game shows) or playing computer games can be very beneficial when you're feeling unproductive or swamped. I'm an "X-Files" junkie, and

I've made it a habit to videotape the show whenever I can't watch it. When I've decided my day is over and I can watch television in bed, I pop in my "X-Files" tape and it takes me completely away from everything that has to get done the next day. Believe it or not, it even helps me sleep. Since I don't have the luxury of a live-in family to take me away from the pressures of my business, I often rely on the tube to distract me.

I do recommend trying something physical before turning on the TV, but whatever works for you is your answer. Many say gentle exercise such as yoga or tai chi will help take stress away, relax your muscles and help prevent stress-related illness. When you're under stress, not only is your productivity affected, but your health is likely to suffer, as well. Establish a practice that helps you relax so that you can stop that stressful feeling before it goes too far and takes you into downward spiral.

On feeling adrift at sea

The fact that you work from home is the reason why you need to build these extra little breaks into your week. Those who work outside the home generally have coffee breaks, meetings, even traffic to break up their day. These breaks give workers "people contact," and usually some social connection. That social contact seasons your meal and can add another dimension to an otherwise intensely business-oriented project.

But when you work at home, you don't have those kinds of diversions, so you need to create them. Whether it's a hot bath, or a cold shower, or something physical to get you out of the office, your psyche needs a time-out. You have to provide yourself with distractions to desensitize you or de-stress you, so you can come back to your work in a new unit of time. Doing something that requires your brain to be focused will help you get back to the task at hand.

Working at home is at least as stressful, if not more so, than working in a traditional environment, but in "corporate America," you at least had social contact. You went out to lunch with members of your department, you brought your coffee mugs to meetings, you planned a co-worker's birthday or promotion celebration. At home, all that just doesn't happen. You're left to your own devices.

One of the biggest problems that HBB businesspeople encounter is lack of physically social contact with others. You certainly have telephone social contact—the telephone is your best friend. Your computer is your closest friend, and your most reliable friend is often the refrigerator! These are the foibles of working alone.

The loneliness factor is one of the biggest areas of concern for new home-based workers. (See Chapter 2.) The good news is that as more and more people go the work-at-home route, the bigger your potential social network can become. Other people who also work at home can be your best source for that essential social contact. They may not necessarily be in the same business as yours—it may be a peripheral business— but they may have some of the same problems and successes you're having. Develop that network to share in both the problems and the successes.

Now's a good time to get involved with a home business association. There are many out there, some regionally, nationally or industry-based, and countless numbers on the Internet. The right business association can help you identify and deal with the pitfalls and benefits of your chosen field.

Your clients can also help grease your social wheels. Since I've been working at home, I've developed a different type of relationship with my clients, and they have a different appreciation for what I do. Clients can become your friends, but you do have to be careful to treat them professionally. Approaching a client with, "Gee, I'm really lonely. Do you want to go to the movies with me?" is probably not a wise idea if you want to continue to keep them as a client. Know where to draw the line so that everyone involved is comfortable with the relationship.

One of the secrets to combating loneliness in an HBB situation is to develop interests and hobbies that take you out of the house and among other people who are enthusiastic about the same things. Do you play an instrument? Check out the community band. Like to learn how to swing dance? Courses are being taught in schools and community centers nationwide, all year long. Now's the time to indulge that side of you that wants to learn something new or participate in something you enjoy.

Of course, family and friends can also become a different, positive focus for you. Discuss with them your emotional state and ask for their help. Remember, we didn't come from Superman—we all need a little help from others now and then. The people who love you can be a tremendous support network for you now. Reach out to them.

The pitfalls of the home-based lifestyle

In the more than eleven years I've worked at home, and counseled countless individuals, I've identified two major attitude traps that the work-at-home businessperson can fall into. Some can become workaholics, while others can become very lazy about their business. You can avoid these traps simply by being aware of your behavior. Go back to the personality traits for a successful home-based businessperson, which were discussed in Chapter 1: patience, flexibility, discipline and motivation.

When you're not sleeping, closing yourself off from family and friends, and working 20-hour days, often what's missing are patience and flexibility. You may feel pressure to meet certain goals (making a specific dollar figure, landing x-number of clients), but these things can take time. You have to be flexible enough to re-work your short-term goals to fit in with what's happening in your business. You won't be able to work 20-hour days for long without something in your life suffering. That's not what working at home is all about.

The other extreme is laziness, which unchecked can turn into depression, a common pitfall of working alone. Sometimes it's difficult to set goals because the rewards come in different packages than they did in a traditional work environment. It can be very tempting to make the refrigerator or the TV your most reliable friend. When you start making excuses for not getting things done, avoiding work, sleeping too much or rationalizing, discipline and motivation are needed.

Start setting small goals for yourself—"I'll accomplish this by lunchtime," "I'll make 20 new-business phone calls by the end of the month." With each "bite," your motivation will return as you get closer to finishing off that elephant.

The key is balance and awareness. Watch out for extremes. Listen to your family because they will tell you when you're working too hard (or even too little). Remember, you don't have the telltale corporate mirror to monitor your progress, which is how you used to get evaluated. Co-workers used to help you focus, and someone above you helped you prioritize. Only you can provide balance for yourself. If you have business hours, now's the time to stick to them. Only you can dictate what feels right for you—you and your conscience. Trust in yourself, your abilities and your know-how, and you'll find your way through.

Tuning up your one-man band

My mother, a Holocaust survivor who came out of World War II with a fourth-grade education, always told me that learning was the key to success, and to stop learning leads to imminent failure. (She never said it in those exact words, but that's what she meant.) To my mother, life was a classroom, and learning something new every day insured her happiness.

In tuning up your one-man band, it's really important that you stay in key, not only with what you're doing now, but with the goals you've set for yourself—be they business goals or personal goals. In today's technology age, the Internet is a very easy way to educate yourself, and you never know when that little bit of information you picked up "surfing the

'Net'" will be useful to you. You might need to go back to school, to upgrade your certification or to learn a new aspect of your business, but it will undoubtedly be worth it.

Certainly, there are always new things to learn in your choice of business, whether it's a new technique, a new standard of operation, breakthroughs in the technology—even just getting to know someone at the new company. If you make it a point to learn something new everyday, you will always be in tune with your business and your life.

Avoiding needless expenses and other annoyances

There are two extremes to business-related spending: either you become overzealous about being in your own business and spend money like water, or you pinch pennies and procrastinate buying yourself those tools that will help you become more successful. Both extremes are to be avoided.

When you first start your business, you may be so excited that you don't really pay attention to how much you're spending, figuring that by spending more, you'll be able to earn more. Maybe you want to achieve your goals in the fastest way possible. Unfortunately, your enthusiasm can tend to glorify the equipment or other merchandise you buy. This may lead to agreeing to projects that you know won't work for you because you're "thinking big," or taking on a problem client whose attitude you feel confident you can change. Invariably, you come to regret these decisions.

The other side of that coin is holding back, not getting the equipment, space or services you need for fear of financial debt—like my colleague who works in her tiny, over-the-garage apartment. Overcoming a "poor mentality" can be just as difficult as crashing to earth from your "pie-in-the-sky" dreams of fortune.

Even I fall victim to this way of thinking sometimes. After I started my business, for quite a long time, my work area consisted of a coffee table and a very old, small desk because I didn't want to spend the money on the equipment that I really needed. Recently, on the other hand, I've considered getting a new computer when, in fact, I could just spend $400 to upgrade the one I already own. Upon evaluation, I discovered that the new computer would give me way more than what I needed to operate my business.

Right now, my filing space of four two-drawer files is bursting at the seams. If I buy three lateral files, I'll have 40% more filing space. I've been procrastinating and putting it off because I really don't want to clean out my files (which is really another issue, but you get the point).

No one can determine what you need and what you don't need. No one can tell you how much to spend and on what to spend it. If you do your homework and assess where your business is right now, and where you realistically will be in the near future, you'll determine for yourself what works and what doesn't. It may be trial-and-error, evolving over a period of time, but that's OK—your business will change over time. Don't be afraid to value yourself. Like the commercial says, "It costs a little more, but I'm worth it." We all try to be frugal, particularly when it comes to buying something expensive for ourselves, but your time and your business are valuable.

Perhaps it's worth it to you to hire others to handle some of your domestic responsibilities. If so, a cleaning service can be a boon. You can also take advantage of cleaners' pick-up and delivery services, mobile pet groomers that come to you, personal valets, meal-delivery services or hiring others to run all sorts of errands for you. And every now and then, you can ask your family to pitch in and help you out with work or domestic chores—things that will help save you time, so you can work smarter, not harder.

All of these time-savers help you work efficiently and handle your life in an competent manner that's considerate to both yourself and others.

Looking back at your work
Six months into your home-based work life is a good time to stop, take stock of what you've accomplished and figure out if you're heading in the right direction. In Chapter 7, we'll address how to evaluate your HBB and the steps you can take to make it even better.

Checklist 6 ✎

✓_____ Are your projects overwhelming? Divide them up into smaller tasks that you can accomplish in a single day.

✓_____ Make one comprehensive Things-To-Do list, rather than posting several small Post-It sheets. It will give you a sense of perspective and allow your mind to focus.

✓_____ Save the things that you enjoy doing for when you're feeling tired, frustrated or restless at work.

✓_____ Use business hours for "people contact": prospecting, follow-up calls, ordering supplies. Use before- and after-business hours for filing, billing, writing or creative brainstorming.

✓_____ If you're not getting anything accomplished, leave the scene and take a break, returning when you're refreshed.

✓_____ Expend energy in order to redirect it back to your work. Exercise, pace, walk your dog—whatever gets your blood pumping.

✓_____ If you're so stressed out that you're not productive, ease up. At the very least, plan some time after business hours for restful and relaxing activities. Make a list of these for yourself, so you won't have that decision to make during a stressed time.

Checklist 6 ✎

✓ _____ Make friends with other people who work at home to create a social network.

✓ _____ Look into home business associations to broaden your business and social contacts.

✓ _____ Develop interests and hobbies that increase your chances of meeting new people.

✓ _____ Ask friends and family for help when you need it.

✓ _____ Monitor your work time to make sure you're not working too much or too little.

✓ _____ Keep educating yourself, and try to learn at least one new fact each day. Keep a journal to remind you of how far you've come.

✓ _____ Keep track of your business spending with an accounting software program. Be neither a miser nor a spendthrift.

✓ _____ Once a week, write yourself a note about how valuable you are, detailing something about yourself that you're proud of. It doesn't have to be something you've done; it could be something you are.

Notes ✎

Notes ✎

"*Far away there in the sunshine
are my highest aspirations. I
may not reach them but I can
look up and see their beauty,
believe in them and try
to follow them.*"
—*Louisa May Alcott*

ASSESSING YOUR WORK

7

Six months later: How's it going?

OK, it's been six months since you set off on your home-based work journey. Which factors should you examine to determine how it's going? Well, are you profitable? Are you enjoying yourself? Are you glad you did it? More likely than not, your answer is, "I don't know."

You've probably been so entrenched in setting it up and marketing and establishing yourself that you don't even know where you are. Hopefully, you've gotten into a rhythm and, to be optimistic, it hasn't taken a toll on your relationships. One thing is certain: The last six months have flown by.

The truth is, even after more than eleven years in business, until I actually sit down and make a physical assessment of my financials, I don't know how profitable I am. My bookkeeper tells me I am, and somehow I always have funds when I need them, but my brain is not an automatic profit-and-loss statement! On paper, it seems like I'm making a profit, and since my housekeeper comes regularly, I guess I am. There are indications, however, that I'm doing better than I probably realize. For example, I'm able to pay off my charge cards in full without panicking, and the ATM still gives me money when I ask for it!

No doubt, over the last six months, you've had questions as to the viability of the business you're in. One of the questions you may be asking yourself is, "Is this really for me?" They say that it takes three years for a business to be out of the red. If you're in the black steadily for three years, then it's pretty likely you're a success. But who knows? No one but you can determine whether this is something you want to continue. Chances are, where you are six months into the business is not where you thought you'd be—or maybe it is.

What's your definition of success?

My point is, methods for evaluating success are different in an HBB than they are in any other type of business. Traditional work environments provide standard methods for evaluating your success— usually based on how you've benefited the company (and even if you're working from home for an outside company, you'll probably get regular work reviews). But in an HBB, you alone determine the yardstick for your success. Ask yourself some of these questions.

1. Are my bills paid?

2. Am I where I thought I'd be after six months? Am I on the same track, or do I need to change my goals?

3. Am I working smarter or harder than I did in the past?

4. Do I feel fulfilled?

5. How's my weight? My overall health?

6. Am I less stressed, or more stressed?

7. Am I enjoying myself?

8. Do I still want to do what I've been doing?

9. How does my family feel about my business? Are they happy? How has my relationship with my family and/or friends changed? Is this okay?

10. Have I alienated anybody?

11. What have I learned in the last six months about myself and the people around me?

12. Do I like my work space? Is it enough space for me or do I need more?

Answering questions like these, and adding your own success measures gives you a real sense of accomplishment.

Case Study

NAME: Gail Kearns
NAME OF BUSINESS: GMK Editorial & Writing Services
TYPE OF BUSINESS: Book editing and consulting
ESTABLISHED: 1996
ESTIMATED ANNUAL INCOME OF BUSINESS: $40,000 to $50,000
OCCUPATION BEFORE BECOMING HOME-BASED:
Development executive in motion picture industry

When Gail moved from Los Angeles to Santa Barbara, she found that employment opportunities for film-industry executives were fairly scarce. Necessity prompted her to consider switching gears into a career path that was not only an interesting departure, but something she loved.

"For awhile, I worked as an office manager and assistant to the marketing department for the producers of a popular animated television series," says Gail. "Then, I decided to venture out on my own. I faxed out a resume to all the local publishers (taken from the local Yellow Pages), and, lo and behold, I had a call from one of them within three minutes." The company was a publisher of activity books for children in all grade levels. After working there for six months, she met a self-publishing 'guru' who started her on the road to her own home-based business.

Gail says she didn't realize the viability of her business until she sent out her first invoice and received a check in the mail. "I remember saying to myself, 'This really works!' I deserved it, of course. But it wasn't until many checks later that I realized the consistent high quality of my work had a lot to do with it."

Progressing into book promotion for her clients is a future goal of Gail's, and making good contacts and establishing relationships with the media is a constant challenge. She continues to make headway on both ends, thanks to her determination and positive attitude.

"The most important lesson I've learned is that I should have done this ages ago!" says Gail. "I advise anyone starting out to simply believe in yourself. You can do it! Realize that things don't happen overnight and you must plan for that. In other words, don't necessarily give up your day job in order to start your own business—unless, of course, you're financially independent."

Stairwell Press

January 26, 2000

Dear Gail:

HOT OFF THE PRESS!!!

Finally—here's your copy of

A VIEW FROM THE TUB:
An Inspiring and Practical Guide to Working From Home

Once again, thank you so much for being a part of this effort. Please check out your case study on page 140.

I'd love to hear whatever comments you may have about the book, and of course, please feel free to share it with your friends. . . or better yet, I'm sure they'd like to have their very own copy! Have them check their local bookstores and ask for it by name. If they can't find it, you might refer them to our website at **http://www.stairwellpress.com** where they can order it directly.

Hope you like it as much as I do! Thanks again for your contribution.

409 N. Pacific Coast Highway, PMB 900
Redondo Beach, California 90277-2870
(310) 798-2748 • Fax: (310) 798-8950
Website: http://www.stairwellpress.com

Time to become a non-home-based business?

Here's a good place and time to consider expanding into a non-home-based business. If you need to, this may be a good time to add employees. Or maybe the home-based office simply doesn't work for you because of your lifestyle or the needs of other household members. Perhaps you're having difficulty pulling yourself away from work after business hours, or you dislike having customers traipse through your home. There are many reasons to consider renting office space outside your home. Once again, only you can decide if this is the right move for you.

One reason that should never compel you to rent outside office space is the feeling that you're not really a legitimate business if you're working at home. The goal of an HBB is not necessarily to become a non-home-based business. You can be quite successful and work from home for decades, growing all the while. I'm living proof!

If it is time for you to move your operation outside the home, be sure you find the right space for you. Consider all the factors, including costs, commuting, social contact, location and aesthetics before making a final decision.

How have you matched your goals?

You may need another six months to evaluate your situation before you can answer any of the above questions. Maybe you've just figured out your "niche." Or perhaps you're feeling pressure to return to the traditional work force.

About six months after I left my job and started my business, my old employer offered me double my former salary to give it all up and return to his employ. Even though he was offering me more money than I was making on my own at the time, I turned him down. Why? I reminded myself of the stress and tension that I had been under while working for that company, and I just couldn't do it. Believe me, the security of that salary was really tough to give up, but I'm glad I did.

When you start your own business, you really start thinking about how you want to structure your life. Rather than focusing on money or titles or the corner office, you begin to ask yourself if you're enjoying your life and you begin to make that your priority. It's truly a mind- and soul-expanding experience. So, when you're evaluating your progress after six months on your own, ask yourself what your priorities are and whether or not you're satisfied in those areas. The answer to that question, more than any dollar figure, will help you decide what to do next.

I will say that once you've made the commitment to start an HBB, you really need to stick with it because there will be ups and downs. After I moved to Redondo Beach and tripled my mortgage, my clientele unexpectedly dropped 65 percent from normal attrition. Talk about struggling! But determination and perseverance prevailed.

Pressure to succeed from family and friends may make you waiver in your resolve—or it may make it firmer. Remember that there could be some jealousy among former colleagues who don't really want you to succeed on your own. Whether or not you choose to continue your HBB, remember that returning to a paycheck situation doesn't mean you're a failure. What it means is that you've made a choice in your life. If you never take a risk, you'll always wonder what it would have been like. At least you gave it a go. It may not be for you, and if not, that's okay. Maybe it will be again, somewhere down the road.

Case Study

NAME: Karen Thomas
NAME OF BUSINESS: A Bridal Boutique
TYPE OF BUSINESS: Designer, dressmaker and alterations, specializing in custom bridal
ESTABLISHED: 1987
ESTIMATED ANNUAL INCOME OF BUSINESS: $40,000 to $60,000
OCCUPATION BEFORE BECOMING HOME-BASED:
Worked in the travel industry
REASON FOR BECOMING HOME-BASED: "So I didn't have to answer to anyone or report to anyone on a daily basis. I wanted more freedom in my career and in life."

A native Australian who began her home-based journey "down under" and then moved to the United States two years later, Karen has certainly learned to roll with the punches. Upon settling in the States, she quickly discovered a market for custom bridal gowns and accessories and worked to make a name for herself in that market.

"I got into it because custom bridal was what was needed here," she explains. "You do what you need to do to pay the bills, and you have to make choices."

Before long, her business was booming, and Karen soon tired of customers trampling through her home all the time. She decided to move her operation to a retail environment, renting space above a shop in a quaint part of town. Within two years, her business had grown to such a degree that she was able to again move her business to a charming street-level storefront, in the same area. "I've been in this location 18 months now," she explains, "and because it's so much larger, I've added a number of accessory lines to compliment my dress designs." While the arrangement works for her, Karen longs to return to a home-based business, ideally living in a home with a storefront for her business.

"I would go home in a minute if my husband and I could find the right location," she admits. "One of my biggest frustrations is I can't do the laundry while I'm working!"

While she loves what she does and is quite successful at it, Karen relates that the bridal industry is stressful because she's working with emotional brides and their equally emotional friends and families, plus the work is extremely deadline-oriented. Her ideal situation would be to own a shop that sells her own designs, which she could develop and complete at her own pace.

"It's great when brides tell me, 'You made my wedding perfect,' but I don't like being relied upon so much," she says. "Once, right before a holiday weekend, a bride had come in for a final fitting and had inadvertently left her wedding shoes in my shop. I went away for the weekend, and when I returned there were ten frantic messages from her on my machine asking where her shoes were. I can't remember everything, but because I'm alone here, I have to."

It took Karen about five years to build up a solid clientele, and recommends allowing yourself time to build up a base, particularly if you don't advertise—which she doesn't. "I work on the referral system, but if you're going to advertise, you're going to have to allot money for that and it's expensive. You can't just sit there and wait for people to come by. You have to know who your clients are and where you're going to find them."

Moving on: What's the next step?

The best advice I can give you now is to keep on truckin', keep on doing what you're doing. Maybe the next step is moving your business out of your home, expanding, changing it from what it's been so that you have more or less of what you originally wanted. Or maybe it means you've given it your all and it hasn't worked for you. Wherever you find yourself at the end of this period of evaluation—wherever that might be— be sure to recognize all of the positive changes that have taken place. It's really easy to look at the failures, the things that didn't work out on the surface, the problem areas. It can be more difficult to identify what went right.

Here's an idea that will really pull it all into focus for you. Take a sheet of paper and write down all of the good things that took place since you started working from home. What did you learn about yourself? Maybe you completed a project in less time than you allotted yourself. Maybe you learned you're not cut out to work at home, or your home space is not cut out for work. Maybe being in your own business is still a viable option, but not from home. If you're working from home for another company, perhaps this is the time to strike out on your own now that you've tested the waters.

Remember that being a successful business at home is not negated by the length of time you've been in business or by how many employees you have or how much money you're making. Success is not necessarily determined by being in a luxurious office building somewhere. Success is individual. Your measure of it will probably be different from mine. But if you've met the goals that you set out to meet for yourself, then you certainly can consider yourself successful.

I've just celebrated eleven years in my own home-based business, and I consider myself very successful. I hope this journey will prove successful for you, as well!

Checklist 7 ✎

✓_____ Write down all the elements that would make your business successful for you: profit, lifestyle, freedom, etc. Rate these elements on a scale of one to ten, based on how you feel after six months in business. Evaluate your results. Compare these results to your expectations. Don't be so critical!

✓_____ Create a pro/con list on changing your HBB into a non-home-based business. Will this work for you?

✓_____ List all the positive changes that have taken place over the past six months.

✓_____ Make a date to do another full evaluation six months from now, and continue to do them for as long as you are in business. Think of them as your "work reviews," and take them just as seriously. Point out areas that could be improved, and set new goals for yourself. This practice will help you continue to grow and prosper in business for many years to come!

Notes ✎

Notes ✎

*"If we all did the things
we are capable of doing,
we would literally
astound ourselves."*
—Thomas Alva Edison

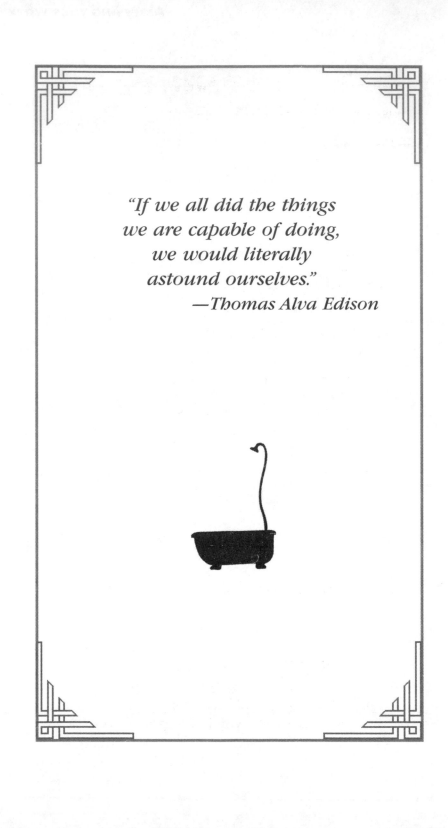

FINE TUNING YOUR BUSINESS

8

After evaluating your first six months in business from all possible angles, you're most likely going to find yourself in one of three scenarios. Each is perfectly normal and does not reflect in any way on your future success or failure in running a home-based business or working from home. No matter where you find yourself, I'll recommend several ways to handle the next move that will bring you satisfaction and fulfillment.

The first scenario:
"I like things the way they are."

This is the most convenient situation because you need not do anything except what you've been doing all along. You like the work you've been doing, you like where you are in your business and the people who live in your house are comfortable with it, too. You have enough free time, enough work to keep you busy and interested, and enough money coming in to keep you satisfied. If you find yourself here, you're not going to change anything. You'll just keep pluggin' along until it's time for your next assessment period, which I suggest should take place in another six months. Congratulations! You're doing fine.

The second scenario: "This is not what I thought it was going to be like."

This one requires more action on your part. Maybe you're disillusioned. Working from home is not what you had imagined in those initial days of starting your business. You're not where you thought you were going to be financially, or you dislike the work you're doing. You miss a traditional office setting or the structure of one. You're overwhelmed by the responsibility of doing it all yourself, yet you're not successful enough to hire anyone to help you out. You find yourself out of balance, and you're just not happy. What to do?

It's time to look a little deeper. Do you dislike working at home in general? It's no crime to go back into the traditional work force. You tried your best, gave it your all, and it just isn't right for you. Others will respect you for having given it a shot (and many will be envious of you for having the courage to do what they secretly want to do!). The next step is clear: take down your shingle and start looking for a job outside the home. You might approach this next position with renewed vigor and from a different perspective than you would have before, because you've lived the alternative. That experience is invaluable.

Perhaps you enjoy many aspects of working at home, but you just need a change of environment— another location or even just another room of the house. Are you finding you can't work at home because there are too many distractions? Maybe you're too tempted to watch soap operas, or the kitchen is too close to your work space and you're eating all day long. Whatever the reason, if you want to (or have to) keep working at home, but you just need to make some adjustments, I suggest you go back to Chapter 1 and review it. The exercises in that chapter will help you hone in on the areas that need adjusting, and show you what to do to fix them.

Another possibility is that you're at a crossroads: you've had an offer from a client or colleague to come work for them full time. The security of a full-time position can be very tempting if you're not completely satisfied with what you're doing. Before accepting the offer, however, I recommend you start back at square one and ask yourself some questions. What do you like about your business? What are your goals? What do you want more or less of? Are you taking steps to handle that? Do you want more flexibility with your time? These are the same questions you originally asked yourself, before you became home-based. The difference is that you now have a slightly different perspective, since you've been at it for awhile. Are your answers the same?

Is it time to hire people to do the chores you don't want to do? When you first started working from home, no doubt you found yourself doing everything yourself because you were afraid to spend the money to hire others. But once you've established yourself, your income has leveled off and you have a sense of how much work you can handle, the decision to hire help can be a more comfortable one.

153

Maybe you need to change the nature of your business or even upgrade your image. If you've been billing yourself as a room decorator, but want to be known as an interior designer; or you've been in residential real estate and now want to go into commercial real estate, now may be the time to go back to school and get yourself certified. Learn the latest and greatest of what's happening in your area of interest. When you educate yourself, your knowledge becomes more valuable and you can justify an increase in rates for your services.

Perhaps you need to add another facet to your business. Do some self-exploration so you can hone your skills while paying attention to the times. These days, people in the business world are truly specializing in certain fields. The computer age has created a whole host of home-based businesses, including Web consultants, Web designers and the like who have found their niche. It's up to you to find yours.

You may even need to move your physical office space. My home office is at the top floor of my house, and because of the changing nature of my business, the people who work for me tend to move on to other things eventually. As a result, new employees are constantly trudging through my house. One of my future goals is to have an office that has outside access, so that people who visit or work with me don't have to walk through my home. I'd like to have a separate work area for other employees so that our separate phone conversations are not a distraction to the work at hand. I also hope to incorporate some principles of the popular Asian art of Feng Shui, which purports to allow positive energy to flow more effectively through one's surroundings. So you see, even though I've been working at home for many years, I still need to make changes in order to improve my working conditions. By doing so, my business will benefit.

Case Study

NAME: : Lori Gilfoil
NAME OF BUSINESS: : self-titled
TYPE OF BUSINESS: Fitness instructor/personal trainer
ESTABLISHED: 1991
ESTIMATED ANNUAL INCOME OF BUSINESS: $15,000 to $25,000
OCCUPATION BEFORE BECOMING HOME-BASED: Homemaker
REASON FOR BECOMING HOME-BASED: "It was a good way to capitalize on a personal interest and hobby of mine, and it afforded me the flexibility and freedom to organize my schedule so that I could spend time with my children."

Health and fitness have long fascinated Lori, who began to teach aerobics and exercise classes after the birth of her first child. After several years of freelancing for gyms and other fitness facilities, she found herself being encouraged to become a personal trainer.

"The people who took my classes began to approach me and ask for my services on a more personal level," she says. "In my mind, I'd always wanted to do this, but previously I didn't have the confidence in my knowledge or the amount of time necessary to do it and raise a family. Soon, I realized that if people felt confident in my ability to do this for them, then I should do it."

Lori pursued her certification in personal training, got liability insurance and began to spread the word. Now, she has more business than she can handle, and she continues to teach fitness classes as well. Despite the fact that she's earning more money since she expanded her business, income is not her chief motivation.

"I always used to base my success on my income," she continues, "but in this case I'm not looking at that. I get more personal satisfaction out of what I do. And I love what I do. I can't put a price tag on that." Not needing to support herself or her family with her income alone, Lori is free to see as many or as few clients as her schedule allows. She relies solely on word of mouth—no advertising or public relations—for new clients, which she admits won't necessarily work for everyone.

"If you're looking to start a full-time business with this, you have to market yourself via your clients, local newspaper ads and flyers in grocery stores, health-food stores and gyms," she advises. "You may want to rent space from private studios to attract clients. It all depends on how hard you want to work. Know what your objects are before you start on any kind of strategy."

Among the personal rewards Lori garners from her business are the positive feedback she gets from her clients, the ability to support others and help them reach their goals, and seeing the results of this support. However, there are some frustrations she faces.

"It's a challenge to keep people on track, focused and motivated enough to stick with it," she admits. "I can't be with them 24 hours a day, seven days a week. Eventually, some do give up because they're not committed enough and they're not benefiting from our sessions. It's also a challenge to communicate with people in a way that they can understand." Refuting the latest fad-diet or exercise craze with good, sound common sense is something Lori finds herself doing constantly.

Lori sees herself being a personal trainer and fitness instructor well into her senior years, although she recognizes that she could branch out into other fields, such as nutrition, fitness education or health-club management. "I find what I do much more personally gratifying. It's another means to carry myself into the next decade or two or three in my life, doing something I truly enjoy doing."

When you first started your business, you probably didn't know exactly how you wanted it to work. Now that you've been doing it awhile, you're likely to have a whole wish list of changes. As you've "lived" your HBB day in and day out, issues have come up that needed to be addressed; this is perfectly natural. In order to help you find solutions to these issues, try asking other people who work at home for their advice. As this book's Case Studies show, people are more than willing to share their stories with others, so let them help you explore the possibilities.

The third scenario:
"I love my business; I just want more of it."

Wanting to make your business bigger and better because you truly enjoy what you do (and where you do it) is an enviable situation. It substantiates your choice that starting an HBB was definitely right for you. Now, you're ready to fry some bigger fish.

It's possible that since you've been running your business successfully for awhile, you've discovered how to do it faster and smarter and you have time to do more. You may be tempted to clone yourself so that you can continue to add more to your plate. Here are some suggestions that may be helpful:

First, try joining forces with either another company or another entrepreneur who is in your business. It's a great way to pool your resources and literally share the wealth. If you don't know anyone who does what you do, check out newspapers, associations and websites that will lead you to them. Develop these relationships even though you may never merge businesses. Having someone else who is familiar with the ups and downs of your business is a great plus factor for your "people pocket."

You might also want to look at other markets. For example, if you're a bookkeeper in the dental profession, you might want to expand it to the medical profession. Or maybe you're a manicurist and you want to become a full-scale aesthetician. Think outside the box of what you've been doing and you'll come up with many ways to increase the volume of your business.

If you sell a product, rather than a service, ask yourself which related products you can sell to the same customer base—these are called line extensions, and they mean big bucks for manufacturers and retailers. Think of a stationery store adding gourmet foods, or a vitamin salesperson adding makeup or personal-care products. Perhaps you have a website that can help you introduce a tangential product to customers. Use all the resources available to you.

Another way to grow your business is by increasing your personnel. Hire people and teach them what you do, like multi-level marketing (or network) systems do. Believe me, it's the next best thing to cloning yourself. This way, you can compartmentalize your business and focus on the things you enjoy and do best, while other people handle the things you don't have time for or don't enjoy. It could be as simple as hiring a receptionist to answer phones, type letters and file.

You may decide that you need a new phone system to handle more calls or that you need to hire a telemarketing company to bring in more business. These are great ways to expand with minimal effort. However you choose to do it, keep in mind the following five successful ways to market or expand a business:

KNOCKING ON DOORS OR COLD CALLING—

Take a lesson from realtors, who are notorious for their marketing skills. When I moved to the area I now live, I didn't know anybody. About a year after I moved into my house, a realtor knocked on my door, introduced herself, leaving behind some materials about her services. Without being pushy, she left me with such a nice impression that when I needed a realtor, she was the first person I called. She's now my exclusive realtor, simply because she took the time to physically come to me, and I was very impressed. I was also able to assess her personality, which is crucial in a service business.

DIRECT MAIL—

Targeting a geographical or professional area is one of the most effective ways to use direct mail to market your business. Choose an audience by location or by demographics (age, gender, profession, income), and send them something that will get their attention AND introduce your services. It can be as simple as a postcard, or as extravagant as a surprise package. Direct-mail marketers can help you come up with the right campaign, and you can even compile your own mailing list as a customer base from which to work. There are also list companies that can supply you with appropriate labels or lists, so check out your local Yellow Pages, trade publications, and the Internet for more resources.

ADVERTISING—

You may already be advertising your business in standard formats such as the Yellow Pages, but the advertising I'm talking about here involves newspapers, appropriate trade magazines, radio and television. In order to get some ideas, talk to local ad agencies, and check out businesses in your industry that are already advertising. Find out how successful the return has been on their advertising dollars. Remember, too, that advertising doesn't have to break your budget—a simple sign on your car can be a terrific advertising vehicle!

PUBLIC RELATIONS (PR)—

This is defined as promoting yourself or your product to the people you're trying to reach. Advertising can certainly be considered a form of PR, but PR is not paid advertising. As with advertising, you can be very creative in your public relations. Submit an article on your business to your local newspaper, making sure there's an interesting "angle" or "hook" to it. Give seminars and/or talks to your local philanthropic groups. If your expertise is vitamins, for example, write a series of articles on the benefits of different kinds of vitamins. If you're a wedding planner, start classes that teach people how to create their own wedding crafts. If you're a dance instructor, give free classes at the senior citizens' center. Public relations is about relating to the specific publics you want to reach. These are the people who will eventually pay you for what you do, know or sell.

NETWORKING EVENTS—

These include business expos, gatherings, trade shows, association meetings, Chamber of Commerce meetings and a whole host of events that are specific to your field. Offer your services, set up a booth at the event and show your wares. Display what you do or what you sell in a colorful and eye-catching manner. Make yourself available in a public place. Keep in mind that you may have to buy a booth or spend money to promote yourself, but if you can reach a broad range of potential customers, it may be worth the cost.

Remember how in Chapter 1 you determined who would use your services? Now that you're more seasoned, re-set those parameters. You may find that your audience is broader—or defined differently—than it was in the beginning.

There's nothing better than word of mouth to influence potential customers. Consider setting up a folder of testimonials from people you have enjoyed your service or product. Ask for a letter of recommendation from each of your good customers— stockbrokers and realtors do it, so why shouldn't you? It's also okay to go back to your customers and sell them again. Talk to the people who have utilized your service or product and ask them to be very honest with you on both the positive and negative side. What did they like about your product or service? What didn't they like? This is market research, and you need it to change and grow, to become better at what you do.

When you work for someone else, you most likely will know what you're doing wrong before you know what you're doing right. When you work on your own, people are less likely to tell you what you're doing wrong. You have to be willing to hear another person's opinion, even if you must seek it out, particularly when that person is a paying customer. Getting others' feedback, identifying with clients as well as family members or others in your household, is part of assessing your business. What would they like to see done differently?

Once you've done that, keep doing what you've been doing. The whole goal of working at home is to be more satisfied with your life, to live life to the fullest. I don't know if this is the only life I have ever lived or will ever live, but I'm sure going to live it the best way I know how. I strongly encourage you to do the same.

◆

Checklist 8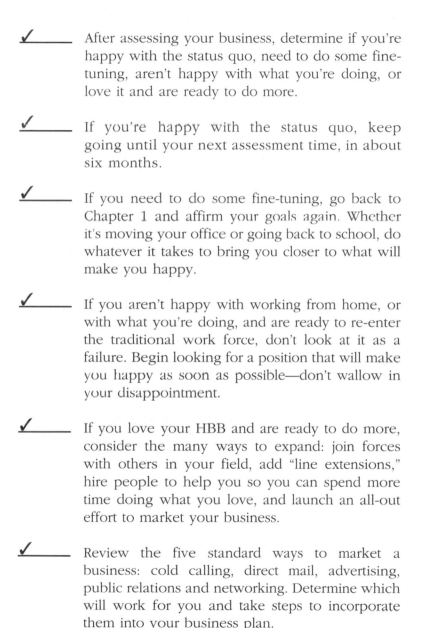

✓ ____ After assessing your business, determine if you're happy with the status quo, need to do some fine-tuning, aren't happy with what you're doing, or love it and are ready to do more.

✓ ____ If you're happy with the status quo, keep going until your next assessment time, in about six months.

✓ ____ If you need to do some fine-tuning, go back to Chapter 1 and affirm your goals again. Whether it's moving your office or going back to school, do whatever it takes to bring you closer to what will make you happy.

✓ ____ If you aren't happy with working from home, or with what you're doing, and are ready to re-enter the traditional work force, don't look at it as a failure. Begin looking for a position that will make you happy as soon as possible—don't wallow in your disappointment.

✓ ____ If you love your HBB and are ready to do more, consider the many ways to expand: join forces with others in your field, add "line extensions," hire people to help you so you can spend more time doing what you love, and launch an all-out effort to market your business.

✓ ____ Review the five standard ways to market a business: cold calling, direct mail, advertising, public relations and networking. Determine which will work for you and take steps to incorporate them into your business plan.

Notes ✎

Notes ✎

CASE STUDIES

Mr. Craig Albertson
ALBERTSON MOBILE MECHANIC
5885 Serena
Simi Valley, California 93063
Telephone/fax: (805)583-5885
e-mail: craigALB@pacbell.net
Preference on how to be contacted: e-mail

Ms. Janice Blair
Santa Barbara, California 93108
e-mail: jblairy@hotmail.com
Preference on how to be contacted: e-mail

Ms. Danielle Bradford
34 Crecienta Drive
Sausalito, California 94965
Telephone: (415) 332-4742
Fax: (415) 332-5946
e-mail: danielle.bradford@tais.toshiba.com
Preference on how to be contacted: e-mail

Ms. Shirley Cornelius
CORNELIUS SECRETARIAL SERVICE
4781 Avalon Avenue
Santa Barbara, California 93110
Telephone/Fax (805) 964-1171
e-mail: SCrnelius@aol.com
Preference on how to be contacted: e-mail

Mr. Rick Cyge and Ms. Lynn Trombetta
MEADOWLARK and LARKSONG PRODUCTIONS
P.O. Box 8783
Scottsdale, Arizona 85252-8783
Telephone/Fax: (480) 481-9647
Website, e-mail: www.meadowlarkmusic.com
Preference on how to be contacted: Website

Ms. Leah Flores
14285 Suffolk Street
Westminster, California 92683
Telephone/Fax: (714) 897-2751
e-mail: leahflores@jps.net
Preference on how to be contacted: e-mail

Mr. David T. Gering
THE GERING GROUP
2380 E. Birchfield Street
Simi Valley, California 93065-2515
Telephone: (805) 526-5599
Fax: (805) 526-5923
e-mail: david@thegeringgroup.com
Preference on how to be contacted: e-mail

Ms. Lori Gilfoil
Little Falls, New Jersey 07424
e-mail: gaglgg@earthlink.net
Preference on how to be contacted: e-mail

Ms. Jennifer Horton
211 W. 92nd St. #11
New York, New York 10025
Telephone: (212) 865-7460
Fax: (212) 362-4183
e-mail: horton66@yahoo.com

Ms. Gail Kearns
GMK EDITORIAL & WRITING SERVICES
825 East Pedregosa Street, Suite #2
Santa Barbara, California 93103
Telephone: (805) 898-9941
Fax: (805) 898-9460
e-mail: gmkea@aol.com
Preference on how to be contacted: e-mail

Mr. Brian Lawrence
SELL THE BRIDE
268 Griggs Avenue
Teaneck, New Jersey 07666
Telephone: (973) 472-1800 Ext. 538
Monday-Friday 9-5 EST
Fax: (201) 836-8895
e-mail: info@sellthebride.com
website: http://www.sellthebride.com

Mr. Kevin Nunley
KEVIN NUNLEY ASSOCIATES
9699 South 2819 West
South Jordan, Utah 84095
Telephone: (801) 253-4536
e-mail: Kevin@DrNunley.com
Website: http://DrNunley.com

Mr. Dan Poynter
PARA PUBLISHING
P.O. Box 8206
Santa Barbara, California 93118-8206
Telephone: (805) 968-7277
Fax: (805) 968-1379
Cellular: 805-448-9009
email: DanPoynter@ParaPublishing.com
Website: http://ParaPublishing.com
Preference on how to be contacted: Website

Ms. Wendy Pratt
PRATT PUBLIC RELATIONS
214 Main Street, PMB 298
El Segundo, California 90245
e-mail: wpratt@earthlink.net
Preference on how to be contacted: e-mail

Ms. Carrie Rossenfeld
1077 E. Pacific Coast Highway, #161
Seal Beach, California 90740
e-mail: cchesloff@aol.com
Preference on how to be contacted: e-mail

Ms. Evelyn Salvador
DESKTOP PUBLISHING PLUS
P.O. Box 460
Coram, New York 11727
Telephone: (516) 698-7777
Fax: (516) 698-0984
e-mail: evelyndtp@aol.com

Ms. Amy Stavis
TABLEWARE TODAY
368 Essex Avenue
Bloomfield, New Jersey 07003
Telephone: (973) 680-4860
Fax: (973) 566-9055

Ms. Marianne Szymanski
TOY TIPS, INC.
9663 Santa Monica Boulevard
Beverly Hills, California 90210
Telephone: (310) 553-8834
Fax: (310) 553-8848
e-mail: marianne@toytips.com
Preference on how to be contacted: e-mail

Ms. Karen Thomas
A BRIDAL BOUTIQUE
4015 Harney Street
San Diego, Califronia 92110
Telephone: (619) 298-2849
Fax: (619) 295-0747
no e-mail

Mr. Arthur Vanick
PICTURE THIS VIDEO and
THE DIGITAL VOICE
1315-18th Street
Manhattan Beach, California 90266
Telephone: (310) 546-5597
Fax: (310) 546-1901
e-mail: avman@thedigitalvoice.com

RESOURCES

Additional sources to guide your home-based business journey:

National Organizations

Alliance of Independent Store Owners & Professionals	612-340-1568
American Association of Home-Based Businesses	800-447-9710
American Business Women's Association	816-361-6621
American Home Business Association	800-758-8500
American Woman's Economic Development Corp.	800-222-2933
Association of Part-Time Professionals	703-734-7975
Employers of America	515-424-3187
Entrepreneurial Mothers Association	602-892-0722
Home-Based Working Moms (HBWM)	512-918-0670
Home Executives National Networking Association	708-307-7130
Home Office Association of America	212-980-4622
Independent Computer Consultants Association	314-997-4633
International Association of Business	800-275-1171
International Directory of Young Entrepreneurs	818-881-1130
International Franchise Association	202-628-8000
Mother's Home Business Network	516-997-7394
National Association for the Cottage Industry	312-472-8116
National Association of Computer Consultant Businesses	910-294-8878
	800-313-1920
National Association of Home Based Businesses	410-363-3698
National Association of Private Enterprise	800-223-6273
National Association of Women Business Owners	301-608-2590
National Business Association	214-458-0900
	800-456-0440
National Business Incubation Association	614-593-4331
National Association for the Self-Employed	800-232-NASE
National Federation of Independent Businesses	800-634-2669

National Home Office Association	800-664-6462
Nat'l Small Business Telecommunications Assn.	410-788-1515
National Small Business United	202-293-8830
Network of Small Businesses	216-442-5600
SCORE (part of the SBA)	800-634-0245
Small Business Legislative Council	202-639-8500
SOHO America/Small Office Home Office	800-495-SOHO
The Small Business Foundation of America	292-223-1103
Young Entrepreneurs Organization	703-527-4500

REGIONAL ORGANIZATIONS

Cascadia Network of HBBA - Washington, Oregon and British Columbia	604-224-7243
Delaware Valley Home Business Network - New Jersey, S.E. Pennsylvania and Delaware	609-784-7268
Home Office & Business Opportunities Assn.	714-261-9474
Rocky Mountain Home Based Business Assn.	303-367-1918
Small Business Network - North Carolina, Virginia and South Carolina	919-556-6808
Smaller Business Association of New England	617-890-9070

National Publications

▲ Home Office Computing   (800) 288-7812
▲ Entrepreneur   (949) 261-2325
▲ Money   (212) 522-1212
▲ Home Business Magazine   (714) 968-0331
▲ Home Business Journal   (315) 865-4100
▲ Inc.   (800) 234-0999
▲ Home Businesss Connection   (717) 361-9007

Websites

➥ isnap.com
➥ members.tripod.com
➥ quailhaven.com
➥ home.microsoft.com
➥ guide.infoseek.com
➥ ivillage.com
➥ home-works.org
➥ nase.org
➥ soho.org

INDEX

174

ABOUT THE AUTHOR...
MILLIE SZERMAN

When Millie Szerman appeared on the front cover of *Money* magazine wearing nothing but a bubble bath, a red telephone and a smile, the business world sat up and took notice. Szerman, 53, who has been running her public-relations and marketing consulting firm New Directions from her home office for the past decade, was enthusiastically celebrated in *Money's* March '96 issue as one of the most successful home-based businesses in the country. The article demonstrated how having the freedom to take a business call in the tub is (or can be) a reality for scores of home workers.

But the *Money* feature was just the beginning of Szerman's plethora of public accolades. In April '96, Szerman was asked to host two online forums on home-based businesses for America Online's "Your Business Lunch" chatroom. In October of that year, Home Office Computing magazine profiled her in a story on paying oneself a salary. The next month, CNBC featured Szerman in an interview about successful home-based businesses. She was also interviewed and photographed for a profile in *Home Worker* magazine, a sister publication to *Income*

Opportunities. In subsequent months, Szerman was queried for numerous entrepreneurial publications and in December 1998 was featured as a talk-show guest on "Let's Get Real," a Boston AM radio afternoon show. In February, 1999, the *Daily Breeze*, a Copley newspaper in the Redondo Beach area, ran a full-page 'Business Profile' on Szerman and the success of her home-based public relations and marketing business. She has also placed an ad in the *Yearbook of Experts, Authorities and Spokespersons*, which is distributed to the media nationwide.

Even before New Directions was born, Szerman's aptitude for home-based ventures was evident. For ten years, she ran Golden Spirit, a profitable jewelry and accessories business, from her home. She even sold Amway products from home during the early days of that company's existence. These experiences have helped her to create New Directions, which has turned a profit every year it's been in business.

Szerman credits her strong sales and marketing background for contributing to her home-based business's profitability. Prior to launching New Directions, which caters to manufacturers of gifts, stationery, decorative accessories, toys and related goods, Szerman sold advertising space in *Gifts & Decorative Accessories* magazine, the oldest trade journal in the gift industry.

Szerman's work and personal experience has led her to where she is today: a highly successful entrepreneur who has the knowledge and experience to lead others down their own road of success. *A View From the Tub* is Szerman's step-by-step guide for helping those interested in starting a home-business decide if they're cut out for the job.